UNIVERSITY OF
MARYLAND

Center for Energetic Concepts Development
Department of Mechanical Engineering
University of Maryland
2140 Glenn L. Martin Hall
College Park, MD 20742
Tel.: 301-405-5205
www.cecd.umd.edu

The enclosed copy of the book, *S&T Revitalization: A New Look,*

is sent to you compliments of

CECD

CENTER FOR ENERGETIC CONCEPTS DEVELOPMENT

Other Publications in the CECD Series

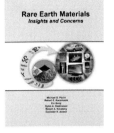

Rare Earth Materials.
Insights and Concerns
Michael G. Pecht, Robert E. Kaczmarek, Xin Song,
Dylan A. Hazelwood, Robert A. Kavetsky, and
Davinder K. Anand
ISBN   978-0-9846274-4-8

Energetics Science and Technology in Central Europe
Invited Editor: Ronald W. Armstrong
Series Editors: James M. Short, Robert A. Kavetsky,
and Davinder K. Anand
ISBN   978-0-9846274-3-1

Simulation-Based Innovation and Discovery.
Energetics Applications
Edited by Davinder K. Anand, Satyandra K. Gupta, and
Robert A. Kavetsky
ISBN   978-0-9846274-2-4

Energetics Science and Technology in China
James M. Short, Robert A. Kavetsky, Michael G. Pecht,
and Davinder K. Anand
ISBN   978-0-9846274-0-0

Other Publications in the CECD Series

From Science to Seapower.
A Roadmap for S&T Revitalization.
Postscript 2010
Robert A. Kavetsky, Michael L. Marshall, and Davinder K. Anand
ISBN 978-0-9846274-1-7

Training in Virtual Environments.
A Safe, Cost-Effective, and Engaging Approach to Training
Satyandra K. Gupta, Davinder K. Anand, John E. Brough, Maxim Schwartz, and Robert A. Kavetsky
ISBN 978-0-9777295-2-4

From Science to Seapower.
A Roadmap for S&T Revitalization.
Robert A. Kavetsky, Michael L. Marshall, and Davinder K. Anand
ISBN 978-0-9846274-1-7

S&T Revitalization

A New Look

S&T Revitalization

A New Look

Davinder K. Anand
Lisa M. Frehill
Dylan A. Hazelwood
Robert A. Kavetsky
Elaine Ryan

Center for Energetic Concepts Development Series

University of Maryland, College Park, Maryland

Cover design by Dylan Hazelwood and Kunal Sakpal

Library of Congress Control Number: 2012954872

Direct all inquiries to:

CECD
Department of Mechanical Engineering
2140 Glenn L. Martin Hall
University of Maryland
College Park, MD 20742
Ph.: (301) 405-5205
http://www.cecd.umd.edu

International Standard Book Number 978-0-9846274-5-5

Printed in the United States of America

Printed in Southern Maryland

DEDICATED TO

DILIP ANIL "NEIL" ANAND

WHO ALWAYS SAID

THIS IS
A NO BRAINER

Preface and Acknowledgements

The issues impacting S&T revitalization and the supply of S&Es are complex and do not usually lend themselves to easy or straightforward solutions. Considering that the United States used to lead the world in the percentage of adults with college degrees but has now fallen to 10th place, and that the outlook for America's ability to compete for jobs in the global economy has continued to deteriorate in the last five years, we need to address this issue and reverse it by a sustained investment in education and basic research to keep from slipping further.

Today, globalization of the S&E workforce plays a powerful role in the education and movement of S&E professionals worldwide. While it is debatable whether there is a shortage in the U.S., it is clear that the S&E professional of the future will be more migratory, alleviating the shortage if it exists. Educational opportunities, professional opportunities and higher salaries are all key drivers of the S&E workforce. While opportunities abound in developing countries, for now there continues to be a large influx to the U.S. of international students and professionals in S&E fields. However, global access to a quality free education from world-recognized and respected universities is bound to change this, while simultaneously creating even greater numbers of S&Es on the global stage. In a shrinking world where mobility is less of a restriction than ever, and where growing economies are beginning to recognize and address shortcomings in their educational systems, the question of engineers becoming a global commodity appears more a matter of 'when' rather than 'if'.

The revitalization of S&T was examined six years ago in a CECD book entitled *From Science to Seapower: A Roadmap for S&T Revitalization*, in which ten recommendations were made. The emphasis in this study was primarily on S&T policy issues affecting the U.S. Navy

Labs. These recommendations were revisited in a subsequent edition, *Postscript 2010*. The fact remains that the total number of students graduating with a bachelor's degree in engineering in the United States continues to drop as a percentage of the total number of bachelor's degrees awarded. With this in mind, we propose to re-examine the issue of workforce revitalization and to focus, explicitly, on the supply of engineers as it is affected by culture, immigration, demographics, and globalization.

Our primary purpose in writing this book is to generate a discussion at the national level regarding how best the U.S. can ensure the vitality of the engineering workforce in the coming century. We feel strongly that our engineers need to be well prepared technically, be connected in a meaningful way to the global science and engineering world, and be gender and ethnically diverse and bilingual in order to enhance connectivity with the global S&E community both technically and culturally.

The authors wish to acknowledge input from Jim Short on export controls, copy editing done by Eric Hazell, illustrations by Kunal Sakpal, production work by Ania Picard and research assistance on various topics provided by Kevin Ray and Piyush Jain. This book is a continuation of our work and interest in S&T revitalization with the U.S. Navy in mind. It is not intended to be an original work, but rather a compendium of open literature. Its purpose is to provide timely information in sufficient detail to support the development of appropriate policy decisions.

The Authors
College Park, MD

Executive Summary

The science, technology, engineering and mathematics (STEM) workforce powers the innovations that provide us with a strong national defense and a high quality of life. Over the past decade there has been much debate from many quarters about the vitality of the U.S. STEM enterprise. Declines in U.S. preeminence in innovation, questions about our ability to meet our national defense needs, and concerns about our ability to sustain a high standard of living have sounded alarm bells. In contrast to the robust annual growth rate of 5.9% seen through the last half of the 20th century, the growth rate in STEM employment has slowed dramatically between 2000 and 2009 to an average annual rate of 1.2%.[1] If the U.S. is to maintain its preeminent position, the slowdown must be arrested.

At the macro level, the United States has seen its position at the apex of global innovation challenged. The U.S. is now ranked 10th globally according to the World Economic Forum's Global Innovation Index (GII), a drop from our position at #2 in 2009—Switzerland remains the top world economy on the GII. U.S. investment in the research and development (R&D) that is foundational for innovation has dropped to 8th; and, while the U.S. is home to 31% of global R&D, this share is now lower than the 37% share in Asia.

At the micro level, as we have outlined in previous books, U.S. employers of S&T talent, including the DoD as one of the largest employers of engineers, face a range of challenges in maintaining innovation capacity. The employment outlook for key constituents of the defense enterprise is that of a "category five storm"[2]—a "bow wave of retirements of experienced S&T personnel;"[3] work environments that have not kept pace with the private sector and academia; and Federal employment practices that hamstring knowledge workers such as those in the S&T workforce. For private-sector employers, the implications of globalization have led to construction of offshore R&D facilities and employment of foreign-born STEM workers. But such strategies are currently not as viable for the DoD which is more "place bound."

Globalization, general cultural issues, and demography affect the pool of talent available to the U.S. S&T enterprise in general and the Department of Defense in particular. Over the past decade, STEM has received much attention, but in this book, acknowledging that the devil is in the details, we focus on engineering, in particular. The aggregate STEM category obscures the unique aspects of engineering. For example, women now lead men on a number of education metrics, accounting for the majority of college graduates. Yet, in engineering, women are still fewer than one-in-five among all new bachelor's degree recipients in the field. In addition, in most science fields, the doctoral degree is considered the entry-level credential for professional practice, but the bachelor's degree–with its far shorter educational incubation period–is the standard in engineering.

A limited comparative approach in which the U.S. engineering workforce is compared to that in China and India provides insights about revitalizing the U.S. engineering career path. As two of the BRIC[4] nations, China and India have the potential to become innovation powerhouses on the global stage. The cultural milieu in each of the three nations has different implications for the engineering profession in each nation. While interest in engineering has been declining in the United States, the field has increased in popularity in both of these nations, each of which is following a different path for building a robust engineering educational infrastructure. In India, for example, the increased popularity of engineering has spurred the growth of private schools that hope to cash in on the demand for engineering education. In China, however, the growth of engineering is driven by state-level policies that have required public institutions to expand their programs in order to educate the talent needed to develop that nation's transportation infrastructure, energy systems, and urban development.

Findings and Conclusions

(1) U.S. engineering has an identity issue and needs to do a better job of attracting diverse students.

Engineering has a general "image problem" in the United States. Most Americans have no idea what engineers do! In a 2009 poll, 49% of respondents indicated that the United States would remain a technological leader for the world in the coming years and characterized five major engineering challenges presented to them as either "high priorities" or "absolute top priorities." In the same poll, though, Americans were unable to describe engineering work, in general, and failed to recognize the key role of engineers in meeting these challenges. Key findings in this area are:

- Occupational prestige rankings place engineering at the top in China and India but Americans place engineering in the middle of most professional jobs.
- College-bound Indian and Chinese students spend more time in school, face more competition for college positions, and, as a group, expend greater effort at academic pursuits than their counterparts in the U.S.
- Relatively few U.S. high school students take the rigorous curriculum that leads to college success and there are important ethnic variations—while 29% of Asian American students take a rigorous curriculum, fewer than 10% of underrepresented minorities and just 14% of white students take this set of classes.

The rich diversity of the United States is a potential strength in the race to innovate, yet the compositional diversity of engineering remains problematic. As the National Action Council for Minorities in Engineering, Inc. (NACME) has shown[5], the U.S. engineering workforce does not resemble the U.S. workforce. Key findings are:

- Women accounted for just 13% of engineers while African Americans were 5% and Latinos 6%[6] in 2009. Yet, overall, members of these three groups account for 61% of the U.S. labor force.
- Women of all ethnic groups and men from underrepresented minority groups currently account for 68% of all U.S. college students but just 28% of new engineering graduates at the bachelor's level.
- If U.S. women and African American, American Indian and Alaska Native and Latino/Hispanic men earned bachelor's degrees in engineering at the same rate as white men, the U.S. could have produced an additional 67,800 engineering bachelor's-degreed graduates in 2010, nearly doubling the 69,900 produced that year.

(2) Reforming immigration rules would result in an increase in the high-skilled S&E workforce for many years to come.

Immigration has been a critical process in enabling economic growth and prosperity of the United States[7]. The largest immigrant groups today are from Asia and Latin America, who, like previous immigrants, are often enterprising individuals attracted by economic opportunities.

- 61% of Asian immigrant adults (aged 25 to 64) have at least a bachelor's degree, twice the rate of non-Asian immigrants, making recent Asian arrivals the most highly educated cohort of immigrants in U.S. history.[8]
- The immigration visa process has become a major bottleneck in providing additional skilled foreign nationals to supplement our domestic supply of scientists and engineers.

High-skill immigrants enrich our engineering enterprise and provide meaningful connections to the global marketplace for ideas.

(3) There is increasingly intense international competition for skilled S&T workers.

Finally, the world has become flatter. Increasingly rapid communications and transportation mean today's workers compete with workers from all over the world—this is especially true of knowledge workers like engineers. Key findings about globalization include:

- New online flexible educational enterprises (e.g., Massive Open Online Courses and the Khan Academy) are leveling the worldwide educational playing field. Open global access to a high-quality free education from world-recognized and respected universities is likely to create greater numbers of S&E's on the global stage.
- Globalization has helped fuel significant growth in the migration of high-skill technical talent. With digital access to vast resources of information and growing communication networks, engineering has been transformed into a global and 'outsourceable' endeavor.
- Antiquated export control rules and regulations (ITAR and EAR) need to be modified and clarified for future international trade and R&D, due to overly broad coverage of what are considered to be restricted technologies.
- U.S. engineers need the full 21st century skills toolbox to effectively compete in engineering work environments, which often cross multiple international boundaries.

Recommendations

Based on our findings and conclusions, we propose a set of eight key recommendations for actions necessary at a national level to revitalize the U.S. engineering workforce.

1) Monitor progress of the American COMPETES Act.

- The NSF's National Center for Science and Engineering Statistics (NCSES, formerly Science Resource Statistics) should be charged with monitoring the indicator data associated with COMPETES and the *Rising Above the Gathering Storm* report.
- The National Science Board in collaboration with the Defense Science Board and the President's Council of Advisors on Science and Technology (PCAST) should be tasked with reviewing data on a regular basis and reporting their findings to Congress.

2) Expand the role of the National Science Foundation in K-12 STEM education.

NSF in collaboration with DOED should create a pilot national STEM education center – akin to the engineering research centers. The Center could:

- Establish K-12 STEM teacher training and certification.
- Provide on-going professional development for STEM teachers.[9]
- Promote and disseminate high-quality pedagogical research on STEM education.

The Department of Defense could take a leadership role in developing this center in affiliation with one of its educational institutions as a pilot program that could later be expanded to regional centers throughout the country.

3) Encourage professional engineering societies to take a lead role in engineering messaging, engagement at the high school level, and diversifying the workforce. Professional societies should:

- Encourage engineering as a profession of choice for young students through improved messaging.

- Establish high school chapters similar to those at colleges and universities to provide meaningful connections among high school students, college engineering students and professional engineers.
- Ensure that organizational strategic plans and national platforms explicitly embrace diversity.

4) Encourage efforts to develop virtual academies for STEM subjects, such as the Khan Academy.

The National Science Foundation, Department of Education, ONR, and others should encourage virtual STEM academy content development as a cooperative activity with our international partners. These entities should take a lead in developing assessment and "consumer guides" for the programs.

5) Streamline the visa process for foreign S&T students and professionals.

- Increase careful evaluation of, and emphasis on, high-demand STEM skills for visa applicants.
- Reduce wait-times.

6) Actively develop underrepresented group representation in pathways to engineering careers.

- Engineering colleges should create a senior administrative position, with appropriate budget and staff support, to increase the presence of groups traditionally underrepresented in engineering.
- DOD's National Defense Education Program Science, Mathematics, and Research for Transformation (SMART) initiative should be expanded to emphasize these scholarships-for-service to increase participation in engineering by underrepresented groups.

7) Require states to pursue a stronger role for community colleges.

- Monitor and increase the efficacy of articulation agreements to provide students with a true pathway from the two-year to four-year degree.
- States should mediate program development so that two year STEM programs are co-developed with four year institutions to allow an easier transition.

- Develop dual enrollment programs so that students form an early connection to both the two-year and the four-year institutions.
- Implement state-level articulation agreements rather than ones that are forged between two institutions.

8) Benchmark U.S. STEM education against high performing OECD countries, and provide funding for rigorous evaluation of STEM education.

U.S. STEM education performance should be benchmarked against high performing OECD countries. Education expenditure adjustments should be made as appropriate to the end goal of performing at or exceeding the levels in these countries. As a key component of this effort, a comprehensive examination of current STEM expenditures should be undertaken. Efforts are already underway to increase accountability for public funds expenditures, among which are included education expenditures. New guidance from the Office of Management and Budget, for example, indicates that Federal agencies should be using evidence and evaluation to improve programmatic performance and as a basis for making decisions about programs on an on-going basis. Recent guidance from the General Accountability Office as well as the competitive i3 grants that have been funded by the DOED in the past couple of years underscore the role of high-quality, rigorous evaluation as a means to improve education. STEM education should be subjected to careful assessment and evaluation, with sufficient funding provided for independent assessments and evaluations.

9) The President should issue an Executive Order that requires engagement of Federal scientists and engineers in the global S&T community.

The challenges of globalization run head-long into Federal work rules and practices that make it nearly impossible for Federally-employed S&Es to keep up with their fields. Yet international experiences are becoming even more prevalent in other sectors (i.e., academia and private-sector). Our entire cadre of Federal scientists and engineers working at the frontiers of science and technology innovation should attend at least one conference outside the U.S. every two years, with a further requirement to inform others on international R&D efforts. As a result we will have a global S&T awareness network capable of providing early warning of disruptive technologies, which might impact our economy and/or our defense posture. It is imperative that our federal technical establishment be a full and equal player in the global S&T community.

References

1. National Science Foundation (2012). *Science and Engineering Indicators 2012*. NSB 12-01. Alexandria, VA.
2. Rising above the Gathering Storm Committee (2010). *Rising Above the Gathering Storm, Revisited: Rapidly Approaching Category 5*. National Academies Press, Washington D.C.
3. Kavetsky, R., Marshall, M. and Anand, D.K. (2010). *From Science to Seapower: A Roadmap for S&T Revitalization. POSTSCRIPT 2010*. CALCE EPSC Press, University of Maryland, College Park, MD.
4. Brazil, Russian Federation, India and China are the "BRIC" nations. These four economies have large populations and have been making investments in the educational infrastructure necessary to grow engineers and to support highly-advanced research and development.
5. Frehill, L.M. (2011). *2011 NACME DATABOOK, A comprehensive Analysis of the 'New' American Dilemma*, National Action Council on Minorities.
6. Frehill, L.M. (2010). *Fact Sheet: U.S. Engineering Work Force* White Plains, NY: NACME, Inc. Note: "All engineering occupations" includes "engineering managers," "engineers," "engineering technicians," and "sales engineers."
7. Lieberson, S. (1981). *A Piece of the Pie: Blacks and White Immigrants since 1880*. University of California Press, Berkeley, CA.
8. Pew Research Center (2012). "The Rise of Asian Americans", Social and Demographic Trends, Pew Research Center, June 19, 2012, p. 1.
9. National Research Council (2012). *Monitoring Progress Toward Successful K-12 STEM Education: A Nation Advancing?* prepublication copy, National Academies Press, Washington, DC.

Author Biographies

Davinder K. Anand is Professor of Mechanical Engineering and Director of the Center for Energetic Concepts Development, both at the University of Maryland, College Park. He received his doctorate from George Washington University in 1965. Dr. Anand was Senior Staff at The Applied Physics Laboratory of the Johns Hopkins University from 1965-1974. From 1991-2002, he chaired the Department of Mechanical Engineering at College Park. He has served as a Director of the Mechanical Systems Program at the National Science Foundation, and his research has been supported by NIH, NASA, DOE, DOD, and industry. He has lectured internationally, founded two high technology research companies (most recently Iktara and Associates, LLC), published eleven books and over one hundred and seventy papers, and has one patent. He is a Distinguished Alumnus of George Washington University, and was awarded the Outstanding and Superior Performance Award by the National Science Foundation. Dr. Anand is a Fellow of ASME and is listed in *Who's Who in Engineering*.

Lisa M. Frehill is a national expert on the science and engineering workforce. She completed the Ph.D. degree in sociology with a minor in systems engineering in 1993 at the University of Arizona. Dr. Frehill's work focuses on how gender and ethnicity impact access to careers in science and engineering and on international participation and collaboration in science and engineering. She is the author of numerous articles and technical reports, including NACME's "The New American Dilemma," which documents the persistently low rate of minority participation in engineering. Recent research has appeared in the *Journal of the Washington Academy of Sciences*, the *International Journal of Gender, Science and Technology*, *Mechanical Engineering*, and *SWE Magazine* (Society of Women Engineers). She is well known among

SWE members as the lead author of the annual literature review of women in engineering and as a regular speaker at SWE conferences.

Dr. Frehill has a unique background that includes a bachelor's degree in industrial engineering as well as various assignments at General Motors. She was an associate professor of sociology at New Mexico State University, where she also served as the Principal Investigator and Program Director of ADVANCE: Institutional Transformation Program, which sought to increase women's success in academic science and engineering careers. Her pivotal work in assembling a team of experts to develop evaluation, measurement and reporting guidelines associated with the status of women faculty has also helped make Dr. Frehill a sought-after speaker and consultant to many colleges and universities.

Dylan A. Hazelwood is a Systems Analyst with the Center for Energetic Concepts Development, in the Department of Mechanical Engineering at the University of Maryland. He received a Bachelor's Degree of Applied Computing from the University of Tasmania, Australia. His main expertise is in information technology systems and development. As Assistant Director of Information Technology for the Department of Mechanical Engineering, he was involved in information technology infrastructure development and management, high performance computing cluster development and implementation as well as development and implementation of distance learning technologies. Since joining the CECD in 2009, he has worked in the area of energetics informatics and rare earth materials research, and co-authored the 2012 book *Rare Earth Materials: Insights and Concerns*.

Robert A. Kavetsky is currently the President and Executive Director of the Energetics Technology Center, a research and development organization in Charles County, Maryland conducting research and engineering programs for the Department of Defense and other agencies. During his 32 year career in the Department of the Navy he led efforts in hypersonics and undersea weapons, and was appointed the first Warfare Center Liaison to the Office of Naval Research where he established the N-STAR program, a Navy-wide effort aimed at reinvigorating the science and technology community within the Navy's Warfare Centers. Mr. Kavetsky received a B.S. and M.S. degrees in Mechanical Engineering and a Master of Science degree in Engineering Administration from Catholic University. He has co-authored six books, and a wide array of papers addressing both technical and workforce policy issues.

Elaine Ryan holds the position of Provost at Graduate School USA (formerly Graduate School, USDA). She has more than thirty-five years of experience in higher education administration. Having served as President of the College of Southern Maryland for eight years, she holds the title of President Emeritus. She has held a variety of other leadership positions, including serving as an interim president, executive vice president and dean. Dr. Ryan has provided consulting services in areas of governance, academics and workforce development. She holds a doctorate in Higher Education from North Carolina State University, a master's degree from the University of Maryland College Park, and a bachelor's degree from St. Mary's College of Maryland. Among other awards, Dr. Ryan was selected as the CEO of the year for the Northeast region in 2003 by the Association of Community College Trustees and was awarded the 2006 Excellence Award from the National Institute for Staff and Organizational Development. She was a Commissioner for the Middle States Commission on Higher Education and chaired numerous accreditation visiting teams. Dr. Ryan has served on or chaired a number of boards, committees and commissions, including the Maryland Council of Community College Chief Executive Officers, Civista Health System Board of Directors, Maryland Hospital Association Board of Directors, Maryland Governor's Information Technology Board, Maryland Governor Martin O'Malley's Transition Committee for Higher Education, and the Maryland K-16 Leadership Council.

Acronyms

AP	Advanced Placement
APTIP	NMSI's AP Training and Incentive Program
ARWU	Academic Ranking of World Universities
ASEE	American Society for Engineering Education
ASME	American Society of Mechanical Engineers
BLS	Bureau of Labor Statistics
BRIC	Brazil, Russia, India, China
C-BERT	Cross-Border Education Research Team
CECD	Center for Energetic Concepts Development at the University of Maryland
COMPETES	The America Creating Opportunities to Meaningfully Promote Excellence in Technology, Education, and Science Act of 2007
CoSTEM	National Science and Technology Council Committee on STEM Education
CNN	Cable News Network
CSPA	Chinese Student Protection Act of 1993
DARPA	Defense Advanced Research Projects Agency
DHS	Department of Homeland Security
DIB	Defense Industrial Base
DoD	Department of Defense
DOED	Department of Education
DOL	Department of Labor
EAR	Export Administration Regulations
EB-3	Work-based immigrant visa category
ECFMG	Education Commission For Medical Graduates
ELL	English Language Learners
EU	European Union
F-1	Student visa category
FY	Fiscal Year
GAO	U.S. Government Accountability Office

GDP	Gross Domestic Product
GII	Global Innovation Index
GM	General Motors
HCL	HCL Technologies, an Indian IT firm
H-1B	A U.S. temporary work visa
H-1B2	A DoD-specific visa category
HBCU	Historically Black Colleges and Universities
HE	Higher Education
HERI	Higher Education Research Institute
HSI	Hispanic Serving Institution
I3	Investing in Innovation
I-CORE	Israeli S&E program
IEEE	Institute of Electrical and Electronics Engineers
IFEZ	South Korea's Incheon Free Economic Zone
IIT	Indian Institutes of Technology
INA	Immigration and Naturalization Act of 1990
INS	Immigration and Naturalization Service
IT	Information Technology
ITAR	International Traffic in Arms Regulations
IPEDS	Integrated Post-secondary Education Data System
K-12	Kindergarten through 12th Grade
K-16	Kindergarten through senior year of college
KAUST	King Abdullah University of Science and Technology
LCD	Liquid Crystal Display
LPR	Legal Permanent Resident
LTF	Laying the Foundation
MIT	Massachusetts Institute of Technology
MBA	Master of Business Administration
MOOC	Massive Online Open Course
NACE	National Association of Colleges and Employers
NACME	National Action Council for Minorities in Engineering
NAE	National Academy of Engineering
NCES	National Center for Education Statistics
NCSES	National Center for Science and Engineering Statistics
NDAA	National Defense Authorization Act
NDEP	National Defense Education Program
NMSI	National Math and Science Initiative
NPR	National Public Radio
NRC	National Research Council
NSBE	National Society of Black Engineers
NSB	National Science Board
NSF	National Science Foundation
NPS	Naval Postgraduate School

NYU	New York University
OBHE	Observatory on Borderless Higher Education
OECD	Organization for Economic Co-operation and Development
ONR	Office of Naval Research
OPT	Optional Practical Training
PARCC	The Partnership for Assessment of Readiness for College and Careers
PCAST	President's Council of Advisors on Science and Technology
PISA	Program for International Student Assessment
PLTW	Project Lead The Way
R&D	Research and Development
SASS	Schools and Staffing Survey
S&E	Science and Engineering
S&Es	Scientists and Engineers
S&T	Science and Technology
SAT	Scholastic Aptitude Test (standardized test for U.S. college admission)
SES	Socioeconomic Status
SESTAT	Scientists and Engineers Statistical Data System
SET	Science, Engineering and Technology
SHPE	Society of Hispanic Professional Engineers
SKIL	S:1348: Comprehensive Immigration Reform Act of 2007
SMART	Department of Defense's National Defense Education Program Science, Mathematics, and Research for Transformation
STEM	Science, Technology, Engineering and Mathematics
SWE	Society of Women Engineers
UAE	United Arab Emirates
UCLA	University of California, Los Angeles
URM	Underrepresented Minorities
U.K.	United Kingdom
U.S.	United States
USCIS	U.S. Citizenship and Immigration Services
UCL	University College London
USSR	The Union of Soviet Socialist Republics
VDI	Association of German Engineers
VDP	Virginia Demonstration Project

Contents

List of Figures

List of Tables

Chapter 1

Introduction

"America is the one country in the world that doesn't seem to recognize that it's in competition for the great minds and the capital of the world."[1]

Since the National Academies' publication of *Rising Above the Gathering Storm*[2] in 2005, the nation has been abuzz with concern about science, technology, engineering and mathematics (STEM). Most states have established a STEM office or coordinating committee; at the Federal level there are STEM coalitions, caucuses and the Office of Science and Technology Policy's Co-STEM (Committee on STEM). To match this plethora of STEM entities, there are many definitions of the term and of the disciplines it includes. The political ramifications of being "counted" as STEM are significant, as those in the policy arena suggest that teachers in STEM should earn higher salaries than those not in STEM, for example.

We suggest that the term, STEM, is too broad, aggregating too many disparate elements, precluding detailed, meaningful analysis. Many of the treatments discuss STEM without regard to the constituent disciplines or degree fields nor the broad labor market outcomes and long-term career trajectories of degree recipients – regardless of whether those treatments refer to problems on the supply-side of the labor equation. In addition, in many of the debates on the topic, little attention is paid to the connection between degree levels and types of STEM work. By aggregating a richly diverse set of fields into the "STEM" category, the more complex connections between educational preparation and labor market careers are not adequately considered within the supply/demand debates.[3]

Our work drills down into the STEM fields to focus on engineers as a particular type of workforce need in the United States within a cross-national perspective. While basic science may move elsewhere, as Hill asserts, engineers as "translators and exploiters of new science" – an expanding labor market in post-scientific society according to Hill – are likely to be in increasing demand in the United States. Current demand signals suggest that this is the case. Even during the most recent recession, engineers' unemployment rates were lower than those of the workforce at large – about 6 percent rather than 9 percent – and among new bachelor's degree recipients, engineers continue to post some of the largest average starting salaries.[4]

Juxtaposed to the alarm in *Rising Above the Gathering Storm* and its sequel *Now Approaching Category 5*[5], a number of key science and engineering workforce analyses have questioned the underlying conclusion that there are too few people in STEM to insure the vitality of the U.S. labor force. Careful analyses have been completed by Lowell and Salzman[6] (2007) and Galama and Hosek[7] (2008); both suggest that the alarms about the U.S. capacity to grow a skilled STEM workforce are exaggerated. Both studies, however, conclude that we need a more refined examination of specific fields and of the extent to which the supply of newly-minted degree-holders matches the labor force demands. Likewise these studies address, but do not forecast, the impact associated with the inability of the U.S. STEM enterprise to tap the rapidly growing pool of college-aged underrepresented minority students.

> *"The United States used to lead the world in the percentage of adults with college degrees but has now fallen to 10th place. That's partly because we have such a high dropout rate. While more than two-thirds of students who graduate from U.S. high schools attend college or pursue postsecondary training, barely one-third of those will end up getting a degree. Something is clearly broken."*[8]

Other work, on a more theoretical level, by Christopher Hill[9] suggests that the United States and many Western European nations have entered a "post-scientific society" in which fewer scientists will be necessary. Instead, more "translators and exploiters of new science" rather than "contributors to the body of knowledge" will be needed. He emphasizes that in Western countries, the key will be to use new science developed elsewhere.

There is another important demand signal that the field is not producing enough bachelor's-degreed entry-level engineers in specific specialties: firms often hire those with degrees in other, allied fields such as physics or engineering science instead of electrical or mechanical engineering. Another burgeoning labor market in which this is the case is information technology. Despite the chilling-out that occurred after the dot-com bust, the critical nature of information technology as a constituent element of all workplaces across sectors has led to continued robust entry-level hiring and demand. More than half of H-1B visas issued in 2011[10] were for workers in computing and IT, and it is clear that workers in these fields have a broad array of educational backgrounds. Such diversity of preparation suggests that, while education may be important, employers, at least in some cases, acknowledge that on-the-job training can provide the specific technical skills necessary to bridge between non-computing academic preparation and the IT workplace.

> *The supply and demand of the engineering workforce has no national boundaries. For the United States, it must include more minorities, African-Americans, Hispanics, women and an influx of highly trained immigrants.*

We will focus on the engineering workforce and on the implications of the demographic transition currently underway in the United States for the future U.S. engineering workforce. Many employers, including those in the U.S. Navy, the petroleum and nuclear industries, and the larger Defense Industrial Base (DIB), are concerned that the current generation of senior engineers is nearing retirement age, while the supply of graduates does not match the increasing demand. Further, it is often stated that the rise in numbers of both student enrollment in engineering and degree-holders joining the engineering workforce in India, China, and Russia threatens the long-term technological superiority of

America's defense efforts. Based on this premise, policymakers have recommended that a more aggressive program to induce students to go into S&E is necessary and can be achieved by funding a variety of federal programs such as STEM, VDP, NDEP and NSF/Graduate Fellowships. While episodic information suggests that many of these programs may have a salutary effect, it is not at all clear that they would yield a significant number of home-grown engineers or that these federal investments are the optimal way to achieve our goal of a robust engineering workforce.

In our earlier document, we examined the revitalization of the S&E workforce and made ten recommendations. These were visited in *Postscript 2010*. The fact remains that the total number of students graduating with a bachelor's degree in engineering in the United States continues to drop as a percentage of the total number of bachelor's degrees awarded. With this in mind we propose to re-examine the issue of workforce revitalization and to focus, explicitly, on the supply of engineers as it is affected by culture, immigration, demographics and globalization.

America's ability to compete for quality jobs in the global economy has continued to deteriorate in the last five years, and the nation needs a sustained investment in education and basic research to keep from slipping further. The 2010 update of the pivotal 2005 report *Rising Above the Gathering Storm: Energizing and Employing America for a Brighter Economic Future* asserted that the nation had not made sufficient progress since 2005 to strengthen K-12 education and double the federal basic-research budget. The report notes, "while progress has been made in certain areas … the latitude to fix the problems being confronted has been severely diminished by the growth of the national debt over this period from $8 trillion to $13 trillion." Moreover, "many other nations have been markedly progressing, thereby affecting America's relative ability to compete for new factories, research laboratories, administrative centers - and jobs."[11]

In *Who Will Do Science? Revisited*[12], the author raises some very interesting issues pertaining to the oversupply, undersupply, or impending shortage of doctoral scientists and engineers as well as to the fact that prediction itself is an inexact science. Other work in this vein commissioned by the National Action Council for Minorities in Engineering (NACME) specifically describes the implications of increasing diversity with respect to the nation's engineering workforce needs.[13] It appears that there was even some doubt as to the validity of the models NSF used to make such predictions. Nevertheless, it was clear that there is a shortage of S&Es from underrepresented groups, and therefore the diversity of the talent pool becomes a significant policy issue.

Certainly, a cross-referencing of demographics and SAT scores clearly shows the need for intervention. Data in Figure 1.1 and Figure 1.2 show the increasing racial and ethnic diversity of the U.S. population, including a dramatic shift from the current to the projected demographic composition of the United States. Perhaps the most dramatic of these changes are the steady declines in the proportion of the population that is White non-Hispanic, and the sharp increases in the proportions of the population that are Latino and Asian American. By 2050 no one racial/ethnic group will constitute a numerical majority, with non-Hispanic Whites accounting for 46 percent and Latinos for 30 percent of the U.S. population.

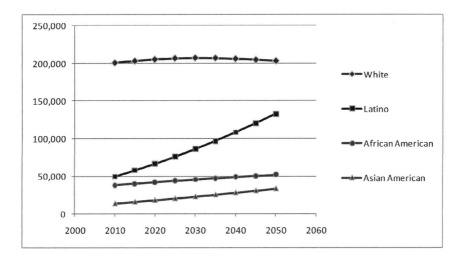

Figure 1.1: U.S. Population Trends, 2010 and Projected through 2050, Select Groups [14]

These demographic shifts are already impacting a number of K-12 systems. Pearson[15] reports that both legal and illegal immigrants have contributed to the greatest growth in public schools since the baby boom. It is estimated that approximately 10 percent of students enrolled in public schools are English language learners (ELL, i.e., English is not their native language). Just as the post-World War II baby boom impacted school systems, so too has the influx of new students now strained many public school district budgets.

"Minorities now account for more than half the babies born in the United States, a milestone in the path toward what demographers forecast will be an overall majority-minority population in 30 years." [16]

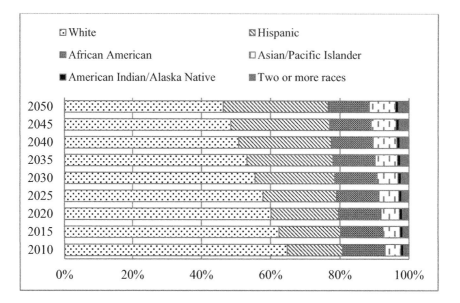

Figure 1.2: U.S. Population Composition by Race/Ethnicity, 2010 and Projected through 2050[17]

Members of most underrepresented ethnic groups are far less likely than Whites to take advanced mathematics and science courses, as shown in Figure 1.3 and Figure 1.4. The gap in science taking is far smaller than that for mathematics. These same data show that Asian/Pacific Islanders, however, take more advanced math and science courses than any other demographic group. It is important to note, too, that the rate at which females take these advanced science and mathematics courses is not different from that of males: the gender gap in high school preparation, therefore, has closed. Availability of advanced coursework varies greatly across schools: those schools in lower socioeconomic areas are less likely than those in higher-income areas to offer these courses.

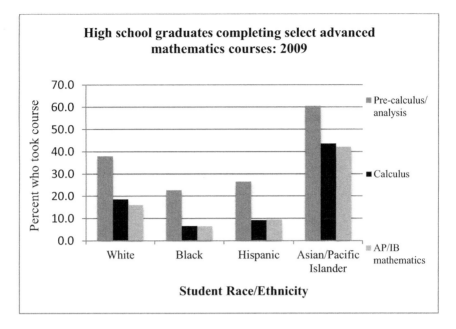

Figure 1.3: High School Graduates Completing Select Advanced Mathematics Courses: 2009[18]

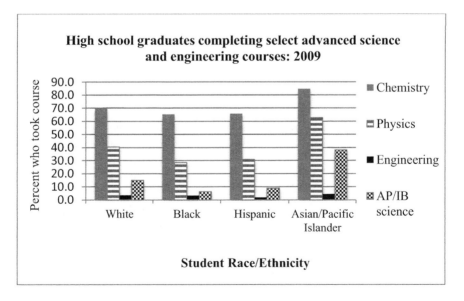

Figure 1.4: High School Graduates Completing Select Advanced Science and Engineering Courses: 2009[19]

These data underscore speculations the authors made 15 years ago. However, there is considerable evidence that these disparities begin early in the educational experience, says Pearson.[20] For example, performance disparities among racial/ethnic subgroups emerge at the earliest entry point in public schools.[21] Although recent studies report performance gains in mathematics and science for all elementary school students, there were not only differential rates of growth but also some widening achievement gaps. Low performing students from underrepresented groups are more likely to attend schools with large proportions of students from racial minority groups, where many students are on free and reduced meal programs, and have teachers who are least well-prepared to teach math and science courses.

> *"SAT scores for the high-school graduating class of 2011 fell in all three subject areas, and the average reading and writing scores were the lowest ever recorded, according to data released on Wednesday. The result from the college-entrance exam, taken by about 1.6 million students, also revealed that only 43% of students posted a score high enough to indicate they were ready to succeed in college, according to the College Board, the nonprofit that administers the exam."[22]*

International collaboration has become one of the many mechanisms by which S&E work is accomplished in academic, government and industrial settings. Most major corporations have developed R&D facilities across the globe to tap diverse human talent – the synergies of which are key in innovation. In addition, major U.S. universities have become reliant upon a steady stream of international graduate students and postdocs to fuel R&D. Further, many universities have taken additional steps with an array of other international efforts, such as recruitment offices or off-shore educational programming, to further tap the international market for high-quality education. Some analysts have been alarmed by the "off-shoring" of manufacturing and R&D work, a view grounded in a zero-sum mentality. Yet it is clear that the world has become flatter and many of the problems that face the U.S., such as energy, water, and environmental issues, are global in nature, necessitating international collaboration.

> *Monetary rewards are key to attracting young people to career fields. But good salaries are only part of the attraction: today's young people place a priority on meaningful work and want to be able to 'give back' to their communities.*

The cultural perception of engineering as a profession is believed to differ significantly between the U.S. and its two biggest foreign competitors, India and China, and therefore affects undergraduate engineering enrollment numbers in the three countries. This perception is contingent on messaging about engineering and the extent to which non-engineers are aware of the work and accomplishments of engineers. In the United States, for example, many non-engineers have little understanding of the work that engineers do. The subject itself has only recently been added to pre-college curricula – according to the most recent Department of Education's High School Transcript Study (2009 data reported in 2011), 6 percent of high school seniors have taken an engineering course. Even in college, though, non-engineering students only rarely take an engineering class. In addition, concerns about the off-shoring of engineering jobs have led many to discourage young people from entering the field.[23] In nations like China and India, though, engineering may be viewed quite differently within the context of economic development, as the concrete civil projects in which engineers are involved are visible as infrastructure is developed and technology solves immediate problems such as access to energy, water, and other resources.

In developing countries, the rise of the standard of living, as a result of economic growth, is believed to have further increased the upward trend in the number of students heading to careers in S&E – as families become more affluent, their children work towards becoming engineers over other professions. Brain drain has long been a concern of developing nations. Now, though, as these nations build their own educational infrastructure and their economies grow, young people are more likely to be educated and work at home, rather than needing to travel abroad to obtain their education.

Western nations, including the United States, have relied on a steady-stream of talented immigrants, especially in fields like engineering, physics and computer science.

Immigrants with S&E skills have been an important labor supply for the United States. In recent years, though, policies that favor S&E as a means of economic development have taken hold in many developing nations. For example, in China, new policies have increased investment in R&D. About 1.8 percent of China's gross domestic product goes towards R&D activities. In comparison, the U.S. spends about 2.7 percent, and India spends approximately 0.9 percent. China's R&D investment far outpaces that of most developing countries and has resulted in increased national wealth. Chinese leaders, for example, are investing more of their vast resources in S&E, and their investment strategies are beginning to be noticed by STEM professionals in the West, especially in the U.S. As a result, Chinese leaders have mounted recruitment efforts to entice Chinese citizens in the U.S. to return to their homeland to assume leadership roles in building a world class S&E enterprise. So far, a number of internationally renowned Chinese STEM professionals have returned to China, lured by generous research funding (among other perks) the government provides. Chinese leaders believe that the status of S&E in China will be attractive enough to retain top STEM students for graduate school and the workforce. Ultimately, Chinese leaders see their country as a global leader in S&E.[24]

Immigration policy and laws have impacted the number of foreign students and workers that are permitted into the United States as a way to address gaps in the nation's workforce. Recently, as political issues have challenged major immigration reform, the H-1B visa program has been a key mechanism by which U.S. employers gain access to non-U.S. citizens. The belief is that encouraging immigration of professionals in key fields can solve domestic S&E shortages faster than attempting to grow our workforce internally, at significant cost. Some analysts have shown, however, that despite the wage requirements associated with the program, H-1B workers' earnings are lower than those of non-visa workers in the same jobs.[25] Interestingly, foreign S&E students receiving doctoral degrees in the U.S. are more likely to stay than those in other fields. Women are slightly more likely to stay than men, and China (89% at 5 years) and India (79% at 5 years) are countries of origin with stay rates well above average. Engineering Ph.D.'s are in the middle of the pack in terms of stay rates of S&E fields.[26]

Consider the case of medical doctors in the U.S. Immigration reform in 1965, then later Acts in 1972, 1989 and 1990, established increasingly lucrative preferences for scientists, engineers and health professionals. In 1976, the Health Professions Educational Assistance Act put in place "qualitative barriers" that required immigrant physicians and surgeons to demonstrate competency in oral and written English, and pass both the Visa Qualifying Exam and the National Board of Medical Examiners' Examination (or equivalent).[27] For doctors, this equivalency test is the Education Commission for Medical Graduates (ECFMG). Many immigrants in this category came from India, Pakistan, and Iran, even though there was a shortage of doctors in their own countries. The lure of higher wages and a freer environment was very strong. This approach did two things – it posed no overcrowding of our medical schools, and it reduced the shortage of doctors without graduating more doctors. In time, many of these foreign doctors became U.S. citizens and are today a part of the fabric of our society.

Not everyone believes that a dearth of scientists and engineers is on the horizon. Reporting for American Society of Engineering Education's *Prism,* Selingo[28] states that a 2004 RAND Corp. study, *Will the Scientific and Technology Workforce Meet the Requirements of the Federal Government,* "concluded that this projected shortage of federal STEM workers is not supported by the data ... For one, the workforce statistics for federal agencies include only civil-service employees who are eligible for retirement, while excluding government contractors, who tend to be younger. The RAND Corp. study also found that federal employees generally retire four to six years after becoming eligible for retirement and that STEM workers retire later than do other federal employees."

A more recent report by the National Academies echoes these findings about prognostications for STEM workers' retirements in the Department of Defense and in the Defense Industrial Base (DIB). The interim report, released in November, 2011, indicated that the long-anticipated wave of retirements had not fully materialized and that even if it did, there seemed to be no shortage of S&Es to fill the vacant positions except in key areas such as cybersecurity and some intelligence fields.[29]

Opinions cover the entire spectrum of this debate, but independent of the opinion that there are S&E shortages, S&E coursework is necessary for the future economic vitality of the country and an educated citizenry. The quality of S&Es and the extent to which these fields are able to attract a diverse pool of talent and offer social and economic incentives to retain highly-talented workers, are more difficult issues than mere numbers, yet these are key to innovation.[30]

In the next chapters, we will develop the key themes associated with revitalization of the U.S. S&E workforce. First, we look at cultural issues that affect the relative status and prestige of S&E professions and shape the interests of young people embarking upon careers. The following two chapters will examine two interrelated sets of demographic forces that impact the supply of S&E labor: immigration and the changing demographic composition of the United States. As highlighted above, since the 1950s U.S. immigration policy has provided preferences to encourage the immigration of highly educated individuals and their families, typically in the sciences, engineering, and the health professions. Yet the new immigration is within a context of a shrinking globe, which has implications for the pool of talent in these key jobs. The fourth chapter focuses on the implications for the S&E workforce of the growth of underrepresented minorities – most notably, Latinos – as a proportion of the U.S. population. Globalization as a general process and as a specific set of forces affects S&E in complicated ways, as we discuss in the fifth chapter. We conclude with policy recommendations – emphasizing cross-sector partnerships and designed for government, educational institutions, professional societies and employers' associations – to revitalize the U.S. engineering workforce.

References

1. Compton, R.A., Raney, A., Heeter, C. (2008). "Two Million Minutes: A Global Examination," Broken Pencil Productions. Documentary Film, 54 Minutes.

2. National Academy of Sciences, National Academy of Engineering and Institute of Medicine of the National Academies (2007). *Rising Above the Gathering Storm: Energizing and Employing America for a Brighter Economic Future*. National Academies Press.

3. It should be noted that the National Science Foundation, which is responsible for producing much of the U.S. data about "STEM," most consistently employs the term "Scientists and Engineers" (S&Es). The most recent two editions of the biennial Science and Engineering Indicators include a crosswalk of S&E and STEM for occupations and degree fields. Another commonly-used acronym for Science and Technology (S&T) is in wider usage in international settings. In this document, we will use S&E to refer to both individuals employed as well as to the general areas of science and engineering.

4. National Association of Colleges and Employers (NACE) (2011). *2011 Salary Survey*, retrieved from <http://www.naceweb.org/salary-survey-data>

5. National Academy of Sciences, National Academy of Engineering and Institute of Medicine of the National Academies (2010). *Rising Above the Gathering Storm, Revisited: Rapidly Approaching Category 5*. National Academies Press.

6. Lowell, B.L. and Salzman, H. (2007). *Into the Eye of the Storm: Assessing the Evidence on Science and Engineering Education, Quality, and Workforce Demand*. Washington, DC: The Urban Institute.

7. Galama, T. and Hosek, J. (2008). *U.S. Competitiveness in Science and Technology*. Rand Corporation. Santa Monica, CA.

8. Gates, B. (2012). *A plan for lifting the success of higher education*. The Washington Post, January 22, 2012, p. B7.

9. Hill, C.T. (2007). *The Post-Scientific Society*. Issues in Science and Technology, Fall 2007.

10. U.S. Citizenship and Immigration Services (2012). *Characteristics of H-1B Specialty Occupation Workers: Fiscal Year 2011 Annual Report to Congress October 1, 2010 – September 30, 2011*. p. 11.

11. National Academy of Sciences, National Academy of Engineering and Institute of Medicine of the National Academies (2010). *Rising Above the Gathering Storm, Revisited: Rapidly Approaching Category 5*. National Academies Press.

12. Pearson Jr., W. (2009). *Who Will Do Science? Revisited*. Washington, D.C.: Commission on Professionals in Science and Technology.

13. Frehill, L.M., DiFabio, N, and Hill, S.T. (2008). *The New American Dilemma: A Data-Based Look at Diversity in Engineering*. White Plains, NY: National Action Council for Minorities in Engineering, Inc.

14. U.S. Census Bureau (2012). Retrieved from <http://www.census.gov/population/www/projections/downloadablefiles.html>

15. Pearson Jr., W. (2009). *Who Will Do Science? Revisited*. Washington, D.C.: Commission on Professionals in Science and Technology.

16. (2012). *The Browning of America*. The Washington Post, May 18.

17. U.S. Census Bureau (2012). Retrieved from <http://www.census.gov/population/www/projections/downloadablefiles.html>, 2012.

18. National Science Foundation (2012). *Science and Engineering Indicators 2012,* National Science Foundation, Arlington, VA (NSB 12-01), Appendix Table 1-8.
19. Ibid, Appendix Table 1-9.
20. Pearson Jr., W. (2009). *Who Will Do Science? Revisited.* Washington, D.C.: Commission on Professionals in Science and Technology.
21. U.S. Department of Education, National Center for Education Statistics (2012). *Digest of Education Statistics, 2011.* (NCES 2012-001), Chapter 2.
22. Banchero, S. (2011). *SAT Reading, Writing Scores Hit Low.* The Wall Street Journal, September 15, 2011, p. A2
23. Committee on the Offshoring of Engineering, National Academy of Engineering of the National Academies (2008). *The Offshoring of Engineering: Facts, Unknowns, and Potential Implications.* National Academies Press.
24. "Rising Above the Gathering Storm: Energizing and Employing America for a Brighter Economic Future", National Academy of Sciences, National Academy of Engineering and Institute of Medicine of the National Academies, National Academies Press, 2007.
25. Hira, R. (2010). *Bridge to immigration or Cheap temporary Labor? The H-1b & l-1 Visa Programs are a source of both*, Economic Policy Institute.
26. Finn, M.G. (2010). *Stay Rates of Foreign Doctorate Recipients from U.S. Universities, 2007.* Science Education Programs, Oak Ridge Institute for Science and Education.
27. Ong, P. and Liu, J.M. *U.S. Immigration Policies and Asian Immigration.* Pp. 45-72 in Ong, P., Bonacich, E., and Cheng, L. (1994) *The New Asian Immigration in Los Angeles and Global Restructuring.* (Philadelphia, PA: Temple).
28. Selingo, J. (2008). *Help Wanted: How Real is the Shortage.* Prism, March 2008, p.36.
29. National Academies, Committee on Science, Technology, Engineering, and Mathematics Workforce Needs for the U.S. Department of Defense and the U.S. Defense Industrial Base (2011). *An Interim Report on Assuring DoD a Strong Science, Technology, Engineering, and Mathematics (STEM) Workforce* (Washington, DC: National Academy Press).
30. Bhattacharjee, Y. (2009). *Study finds science pipeline strong, but losing students.* Science, Vol. 326.

Chapter 2

The Cultural Factor

"Fifty years ago C. P. Snow noted that the study of engineering was not only encouraged, but also respected in developing countries."[1]

Henry Petroski observed that "among the things that caught my eye on a recent re-reading was Snow's remark about engineering education having been held in lower esteem in developed than in undeveloped nations. He noted 50 years ago how countries like China recognized the importance of the Industrial Revolution and how it would be engineers who would bring the fruits of its technology, and thereby a better quality of life, to Chinese citizens. Snow also noted that the study of engineering was not only encouraged but also respected in developing countries."[2]

Engineering has different cultural traditions across different national contexts. In the United Kingdom, for instance, engineering has traditionally been considered a blue-collar profession, grounded in a skilled-trades/craft orientation that emphasizes practice. This is different than the French and German traditions in which engineering has occupied a place of high status within academia, as the proper location for training. The U.S. initially had a strong craft orientation to engineering, but as engineering professional societies and engineering colleges proliferated, the bachelor's degree became the entry credential for the field.[3]

In comparison to other professions, however, engineering has occupied a "middle ground" within the U.S. industrial system. That is, professions such as law, medicine, and religious vocations have traditionally been characterized as "private practice" in which one or more members of the profession ply their trade for clientele with an implied modicum of independence from oversight by non-practitioners.

Engineers, however, with the exception of professional engineers in private practice (a relatively small share of all engineers), work for companies as employees.[4] Current U.S. attitudes about engineering, in general, are somewhat hazy. The results of a 2009 survey performed on behalf of the Duke University's Pratt School of Engineering showed that "American adults admit to having little familiarity with the realm of engineering, giving themselves an average grade of 'C' for how much they know and understand about the world of engineers and what they do."[5]

Three Nations: Many Cultures

International comparisons of the S&E capabilities of the United States with those of other nations are not new. Since Sputnik was launched in 1957, the innovation gauntlet had been thrown and primacy in science and engineering as key drivers of innovation became a focus of U.S. policy. Consider, for example: Immigration policy reforms emphasized the need to more easily permit entry of highly-skilled technical talent; Selective Service Registration provided college men in the 1960s with a way to stall being drafted for military service during the Vietnam War era; and recently the America COMPETES Act has provided many supports for STEM education.

In the past decade, international observers have become particularly keen to compare the United States to India and China, two nations with large and rapidly growing populations in the midst of significant social and economic transformations and which possess nuclear capabilities.[6] China and India are distinguished from many others that might form the basis of international comparison in terms of human resources associated with S&E for several reasons. Both nations "send" significant numbers of students to U.S. colleges and universities for graduate training in S&E, and many of these students remain in the United States after they earn their graduate credentials. They also represent, however, a pool of ex-patriot talent from which India and China draw as both nations continue to build their R&D enterprises. Both nations are also aggressively building their educational and R&D infrastructure and have the world's largest population pools from which to both develop and draw talent.

Like the United States, both India and China are characterized by highly heterogeneous populations with important divisions based on location (e.g., rural/urban and state/region/province); ethnicity; and socioeconomic status (SES). While the nature of SES historically differed markedly among these three nations, within the past two decades, the growth of an entrepreneurial/middle class and long-term demographic and cultural impacts of the "one child" policy have altered the meaning of SES in China's urban areas to some extent.

The relationship between educational systems and the labor market varies across nations and functions in different ways with respect to population heterogeneity.[7] Increased standardization among educational institutions promotes equality of opportunity, efficiently sorts individuals, and prepares young people for the labor market. Differentiation of educational institutions, while still preparing new entrants for employment, has been found to neither sort efficiently nor promote equality of opportunity.

In the United States, education and occupations have defined upward social mobility. Culturally, the U.S. places a high value on a young person following his/her own path for "getting ahead." Such conceptualizations are not consistent with socialist state systems such as China's, nor are they consistent with social systems, like India's, in which the replication of class is expressed as a functional necessity. Within China's socialist system, with its centrally-planned economy, the state often wields a higher degree of control over occupational placement than in free-market systems like the United States. In India, familial considerations are more paramount: young people pursue education and career paths consistent with parental expectations, which are tightly connected to conceptualizations of prestige.[8]

Figures 2.1 through 2.3 show prestige rankings of occupations in the United States, India and China. Prestige is a subjective assessment, yet research on prestige rankings both within and across economies has concluded that this subjective assessment produces reliable rankings regardless of how the question is asked, of whom, and in what context. Indeed, rankings across economies that are at a similar stage of development are also reliable.

In the United States both medicine and law have been more successful in appropriating professional status, with control of entry and certification for practice required by the government and overseen by members of the profession. Engineering, however, has had only limited success in securing professional status, with concomitant lower prestige than law and medicine. Further a study commissioned by Duke University found that "most adults view engineering as less appealing to young people selecting a profession or career, compared with other professions, such as medicine, business, or law. Nearly three in five (58%) adults feel that engineering is losing out to these other professions. Reasons cited for engineering's relative lack of appeal relate both to education issues, such as a demanding curriculum, and to low pay, low prestige, and few job opportunities."[9] Figure 2.1 illustrates engineer's 9th position standing in occupational prestige results for the U.S.

The standing of engineering is dramatically different in India. As shown in Figure 2.2, secondary students place engineering at the top of their occupational rankings with fundamentally the same ranking accorded to scientist and computer scientist. Medical doctor is ranked fourth. The survey covered 15 different regions and was executed in 8 different languages to 6,530 individuals, from a total of 88 schools and vocational training institutes. While this survey stands out from the U.S. and Chinese surveys in that the occupational prestige ratings are from students rather than adults, Arulmani notes in the survey analysis the connection between student attitudes and those of the general population, as "Career planning in India is not a purely individualistic effort. Beliefs and values held by the community play a significant role in the career decision-making process. Career choice is influenced by the attitudes of the young person's family and community."[10]

Figure 2.3, a listing of prestige for a number of occupations in China, illustrates a similar cultural appreciation for engineers as is found in India. While the survey data are from 1988, researchers have found that occupational prestige data tend to remain consistent over time.[11] Electrical and electronics engineers were found to be second only to physicians in occupational prestige, according to the 1,632 adult respondents. Given that science and technology are one of China's Four Modernizations and also a source of national pride, it is not surprising to see high levels of prestige attributed to engineers in this survey.

The higher prestige Indian students accorded to engineering was correlated with both higher interest and with the fact that engineering has the highest level of "parental approval." In the United States, however, interest in engineering has been low, overall, but even lower amongst different demographic groups. A November 2009 study following three generations of students along the STEM education pathway, suggested that "Highly qualified students may be choosing a non-STEM job because it pays better, offers a more stable professional career, and/or is perceived as less exposed to competition from low-wage economies. The potential alternatives could include business, healthcare, or law."[12] Of course, as noted by Margaret Loftus in 2006, having a curriculum rich in STEM subjects is one thing, but getting kids to actually enroll in those courses is quite another.[13] She states, "many high school students don't recognize the value in math and intentionally go in the direction that minimizes the need for it. This goes across the board for all ethnicities."[14]

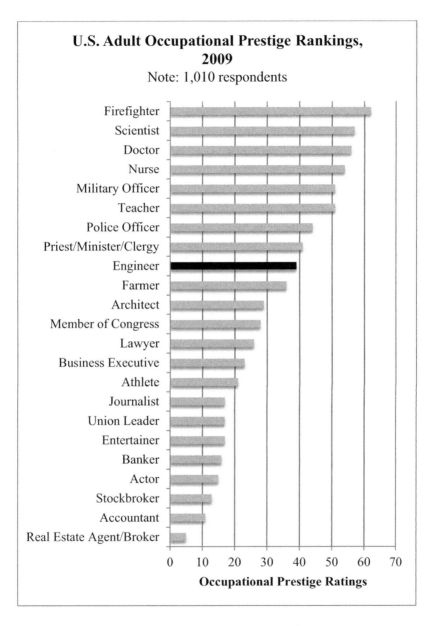

Figure 2.1: 2009 Harris Interactive Poll of U.S. Adults on Occupational Prestige[15]

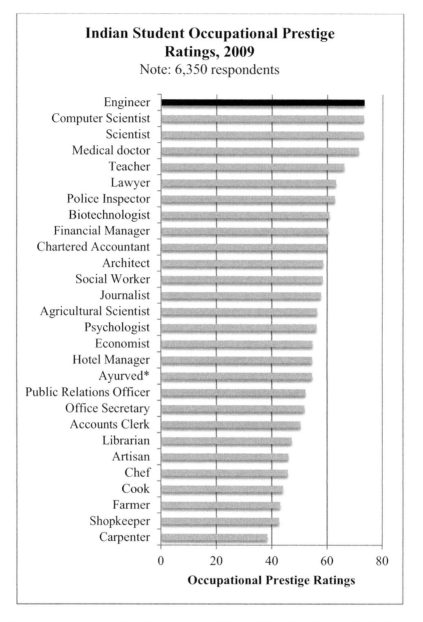

Note: Ayurved is a medical doctor trained in traditional Indian medical science.

Figure 2.2: Indian Student Assessment of Occupational Prestige[16]

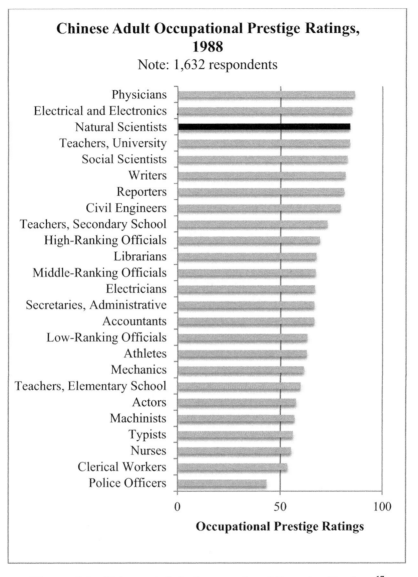

Figure 2.3: Chinese Adult Occupational Prestige Ratings[17]

The differentiation of the U.S. educational system, according to the review in Van de Werfhorst and Mijs (2010) suggests that it is not surprising that the system does a poor job of sorting young people into occupations. Regulatory authority for U.S. education resides at the state rather than the national level: standards are set by states and administered

> *"In recent years, an all-out brawl between school districts and teachers unions has dominated the education debate. Critics of the unions say they're more concerned about preserving their members' jobs than educating children. The unions say that the administrators' reforms aren't doing any good."*[18]

and managed by local school boards that differ greatly in members' backgrounds and expertise. Such a system is in direct contrast to those found in some rapidly-changing (usually urban) areas of China in which standardization increases the ability of educational institutions to identify, sort, and select talent into appropriate labor market positions.

Hence, in the United States, when employers call for and, in some cases, provide financial support for training more engineers, the solutions are to provide incentives at the local level. In contrast, in China, where there is strong demand for engineers to build the nation's infrastructure,[19] educational institutions are increasingly standardized to produce a talent pool capable of meeting this labor market demand. The latter approach represents a system-level response, consistent with an ethos of equality of opportunity.

To get a keener perspective on the forces that determine the S&E posture of a country, we briefly review the backgrounds of members of governing parties for U.S./China/India. For the U.S., the current Senators as of March 2010 were examined; for China, the members of the 17th Politburo; and for India, the Union Council of Ministers. In the United States Senate, from the 100 members listed, 4 members had a background in S&E – degrees in biology, mechanical engineering, and in general engineering, representing 4%. The majority, 55%, possessed degrees in law.

Decision makers in India were found to be from a background very similar to that of U.S. Senators. The Cabinet of the Government of India, otherwise known as the Union Council of Ministers of India, was formed in 2009 and is comprised of the Prime Minister and 35 cabinet ministers. As of February 2010, just one of the members possessed a degree in an S&E-related field (zoology). The majority had degrees in law (48%), and the remainder in other non-S&E fields.[20]

In China, a collection of people oversee the Communist Party, known as The Central Politburo of the Communist Party of China, or the Political bureau of the CPC Central Committee. As of February 2010, of the 25 members listed in the 17th Politburo, 48% held degrees in an S&E field, while 24% had an economics background.[21] These statistics show that China's leadership has a strong emphasis on engineering at the highest ruling level, reflecting the country's overall emphasis on excellence in science and technology. Within the ruling groups of both the U.S. and India, the field of law appears to be the overwhelming background of favor.

United States

In 1994, Samuel C. Florman noted in the book *The Existential Pleasures of Engineering* that the field had a number of problems that were driving students away. "Young people are dropping out of engineering school for the same reason they are shunning it in the first place: The program is laborious and in many respects disagreeable. The 'hands-on' approach is largely gone, increasingly replaced by scientific theory. 'Research' is in while 'teaching' is out, a casualty of the way engineering education has been funded for several decades."[22] In 2012 little appears to have changed, perhaps due to the very nature of undergraduate engineering, according to C. Judson King of the Center for Studies in Higher Education. "Among the principal professions, engineering is the only one for which the bachelor's degree is the primary accredited, professional degree. By contrast, medicine, law, public health, business, architecture and other major professions have graduate-level professional degrees built upon the base of a liberal undergraduate education. Since the entire professional program is concentrated into the undergraduate degree, engineering education has little room, if any, for much needed breadth ... the one-dimensional and almost exclusively rigorous, quantitative aspect of undergraduate engineering education reduces the spectrum of the population to which it is attractive."[23] It is postulated that there are also a number of additional relevant issues, forming an engineering 'culture' that is in need of significant reform given the shifting makeup of U.S. society.

Engineering at the undergraduate level is considered to be one of the more difficult areas of study, and a major that has been characterized as aggressively 'weeding out' those who perform poorly in the initial period of the degree process, in spite of the fact that the number of credits required for a baccalaureate degree has dropped from 144 to 124 in the last 50 years. High levels of student attrition in engineering are noted in the results of a 2010 UCLA study of undergraduates, where it was found that "Only about 20% of underrepresented minorities who aspire to a STEM degree actually earn one within 5 years ... And it's not just minorities who are falling out of the science pipeline. Only 33% of whites and 42% of Asian-Americans complete their STEM degrees in 5 years."[24] The study further notes that, "among students who majored in liberal arts, business or other fields, 73% of white students and about 63% of black and Latino students finished their degrees in five years."[25] Financial concerns, a factor in student attrition, appear to affect minorities the most, with more minorities receiving need-based financial aid than White students, according to financial aid analyst Mark Kantrowitz. "Minority students receive a higher share of need-based grants, representing 48.5 percent of grant recipients and only 38.0 percent of the student population, [because] they are more likely to be low-income."[26]

The culture of Engineering within the U.S., and more specifically the image of the stereotypical engineer, has a popularity problem. For lack of a better term, engineers in the U.S. are generally considered 'geeks'. The 'geek' concept of the engineer with thick glasses, a pocket protector, an obsession with math and science, and awkward social skills is pervasive in popular culture. This cultural perception begins to affect students during high school. As Frehill notes, "The problem is, we lose students by the ninth or 10th grade because kids interested in STEM are viewed as geeks."[27] Unlike young people in China and India, for example, those in the U.S. do not particularly idolize people who excel in math or science within their school. Instead, the stars of the school's sports teams are given higher social prestige. A student at MIT pontificates on cultural differences thusly "In the United States, science, engineering and technology are so negatively presented that most Americans view the typical MIT-type as a hopeless geek. Elsewhere in the world, an MIT-style education is prized to such a degree that foreign tourists, thousands of them every year, visit the MIT campus simply to snap pictures of the Great Dome."[28] In addition, while the American public generally values creativity, it does not associate engineering with that characteristic. A 2004 Harris Interactive poll showed that just 3% of the public associated creativity with the engineering field.[29] It is clear that the engineering field, among others, has an ingrained cultural image problem in the U.S. that will be difficult to change.

The U.S. has cultural subdivisions by racial classification, where each group faces specific issues related to engineering and education in general. These subdivisions are worthy of consideration when examining their effect on students, since there is disproportionate racial minority enrollment in the U.S. engineering programs. As noted by Frehill et al. in an examination of diversity in engineering, "only 4% of underrepresented minorities graduate high school "engineering eligible." For example, in 2002, 690,000 minority students graduated from high school, but only about 28,000 had taken the necessary math and science courses to be fully qualified for admission to engineering study."[30]

At over 50 million people, the Hispanic population represents 16.3% of the U.S. population as measured by the U.S. Census in 2010, and "is projected to more than double by 2050. It's the largest, youngest, fastest-growing minority group in America."[31] Yet Hispanic students are currently underrepresented in engineering undergraduate programs, representing 9.5% of the total students enrolled in 2008, compared to overall representation in undergraduate programs at 12.9%.[32] African-Americans constitute 13% of the U.S. population, and the group's level of student enrollment in overall undergraduate studies nationwide for 2008 was at 12.6%, or almost at parity with percentage representation in the population. However, African-American undergraduate engineers represented only 5.6% of all engineering undergraduates in 2008.[33] Clearly, African-American and Hispanic students are under-represented minorities in undergraduate engineering education. This is discussed further in Chapter 4.

Although beyond the scope of this book, we note that cultural pressures, poor schools and related support infrastructure, family income and support, cultural identity, immigration, role models and governmental policies all play an important part in determining a young person's decision to enter engineering or another STEM field. Most importantly, and common to many young minority students, is the role of poverty. According to the U.S. Census Bureau, 21.6% of all children in the U.S. were living in poverty in 2010,[34] and therefore require significant governmental intervention to ensure positive educational outcomes. According to the 2010 American Community Survey, of the children living in poverty, 38.2% were African American, 32.3% were Hispanic, 17% were White, and 13% were Asian.[35] It has been reported that children living in poverty tend to have parents who may be less educated, may be less involved in assisting their children with homework, may be less aware of the benefits of a college education, and may have less appreciation of the importance of developing an aptitude in subjects such as math and science to support a technical career in a field such as engineering. They may also live in an area where public schools have lower quality teachers, with a poor curriculum, and with less academic support provided to drive children to go outside their cultural norms to focus on STEM-related study. Furthermore, Beegle's study of individuals growing up in generational poverty noted that "almost all of the childhood friends of the respondents were also living in poverty, and there was peer pressure to pay little attention to education."[36] Within such a socioeconomic framework, there is often little hope for young students to develop the proficiency needed for an ongoing education in a technical field such as engineering.

Asian Americans, while also being a minority in the U.S at 4.8% of the total population in 2010, represented 10.8% of undergraduate enrollment in engineering as of Fall 2008. Asian American undergraduate students choose engineering as their field of study at more than twice the rate as their percentage of the general population would indicate. So the question becomes, why has this minority shown high levels of participation in engineering education in the U.S.? The answer may lie in the continuing influence of their traditional cultural background. As noted by Tang, Asian American families displayed a "high orientation towards traditional culture and low orientation towards mainstream culture."[37] As seen in overwhelming enrollment numbers in undergraduate engineering in China, Asian culture appears far more favorable towards a career in engineering than traditional U.S. culture.

Steinberg et al., examining ethnic differences in adolescent achievement, noted that "Asian-American students overwhelmingly believed a bad education would have negative effects on finding a good job, and African-American and Hispanic students predicted few negative consequences of a bad education."[38] Parents in China and other Asian countries have been shown to stress job security and a successful career for their children over enjoyment and diversity of the individual's educational experience, and when those parents migrate to the U.S., those values are transferred at some level to their children. With parents who often have strong math and science backgrounds and a strong culturally tied education ethic, many young Asian American students, unsurprisingly, show interest in undergraduate engineering.

Postgraduate engineering education also has a serious diversity issue. According to Chubin, et al., "Only 5.3 percent of master's and 3.5 percent of doctoral degrees awarded in 2003 were earned by these minority students. This has predictably led to a paltry number of tenured, underrepresented minority STEM faculty (8 percent) … In academic engineering in particular, whether one examines the ranks of those on the tenure track, at the full professor level, department chairs, or deans, women and minorities are scarce commodities."[39] Research by the National Action Council for Minorities in Engineering, Inc. (NACME) in 2008, and again in 2011, underscores the persistence of the problem of diversity in U.S. engineering. The "new" American dilemma is that minority youth are not being provided with the fundamental building blocks for 21st century careers in rapidly-changing fields like engineering.

The engineering field has also not been inviting to women, as evidenced not only by low enrollment and graduation numbers in higher education, but also in low retention rates of female employees in engineering, as noted by Frehill.[40] In *Changing the Conversation*, the U.S. National Academy of Engineering sought to address this situation, focusing on how messages about engineering could be conveyed to emphasize the profession as being consistent with work-related aspirations of young people, in general, and young women in particular. Further discussion of gender issues in engineering can be found in Chapter 4.

India

Following the end of British rule in 1947, a newly independent India was looking to support over 350 million people, a formidable task

> *"In 1951, the first Indian Institute of Technology (IIT) was established at Kharagpur. It would be the first autonomous university, and would operate free from Indian politics. This would prove a pivotal moment in the history of engineering in India. The standard had been set – the best engineers in India would study at the IITs. ... The high level of competition automatically ensured high-quality engineers flooding out to ensure India caught up with the world with respect to establishing an industrial framework for the future. People would repeatedly tell their children – study engineering, get a job and help build India."[41]*

requiring extraordinary engineering resources. The country needed to develop engineers of high quality and in great numbers, and thus:

The IITs in India have undergone growth in both scale and prestige, and are still considered the finest educational institutions there. They are recognized internationally for the quality of their students, and there is considerable competition for placement in engineering: "One of the biggest advantages of the top engineering colleges in India is the high selectivity – approximately 2-3% of the applicants are selected. This is much lower than reputed international universities."[42]

India is undergoing significant growth, both in terms of technology and overall economic development. Growth of R&D expenditure in India has risen from 2.6% of global R&D in 2010 to an estimated 2.8% in 2012. R&D expenditure as a percentage of GDP is estimated to be at 0.85% for 2012, compared to 1.6% for China, putting the country in 8th place globally (by forecast gross expenditure) in a December 2011 analysis.[43] As part of India's 12th Five Year economic plan, to be put in place from 2012 to 2017, the country will increase spending on infrastructure to US$1.2 trillion, with private investment representing 50% of the total, up from 30% previously. With such increases in infrastructure spending, the need for educated engineers is certain to grow substantially.[44]

The field of engineering at the undergraduate level in India is extremely popular, and those who succeed are greatly respected (see

> *"The OECD predicts that by the end of this decade India will churn out more graduates than any other country bar China, giving it 24m graduates aged between 25 and 34, some 12% of the world's total."[45]*

Figure 2.2) – engineering education is in fact so popular that 30% of Indian engineers are unemployed after the completion of their degree, even with very strong demand for good students. This level of graduate unemployment is the direct result of the fact that Indian higher education institutions vary significantly in the quality of their programs. Demand is strong enough that at the best colleges, (i.e. IIT campuses), it is not unusual for a company such as Infosys to simply hire an entire graduating class of engineers. At the vast array of smaller, less prestigious educational institutions within the country, however, engineering programs are often at a lower quality level.

With more than half a million engineering graduates per year, the expectation might be for one to consider India as a global engineer production powerhouse; however, many lack the skills necessary for an engineering position. *The Economist* reports that in a 2011 analysis of 55,000 Indian engineering graduates, 78% had difficulties with English, 56% lacked analytical skills, and only 17% had basic skills. The survey noted in its conclusion that "There is a long way to go before engineering graduates in India become employable."[46] The Indian Government is attempting to address the issue by increasing funding, providing $11 billion for education in 2012, with 25% going to universities (up from 18% in 2011), and 75% to schools.[47]

India's economic direction is based on 5-year plans, the 11th of which runs from 2007 to 2012. The 11th plan contains a number of major recommendations for higher education in India:[48]

- Expansion of access to higher education for "students from backward and Minority communities" due to low participation, with greater distance education development as a key methodology.
- Development of disability-friendly schemes to further improve access to education.
- Creation of new universities and colleges with quality facilities to increase enrollment.
- A specific recommendation to increase enrollment of women – the plan notes that "more women as engineers, lawyers, professors, architects could mould the face of India to a great extent."
- Greater cooperation between research laboratories, private industry and universities to create advanced institutions for science education.
- Promotion of national/international crossflow of teachers/ scientists/students and greater links with international institutions.
- Scientific infrastructure upgrades with easier access to research funding.
- A greater focus on improvement of quality throughout higher education institutions, their faculty, curriculum and infrastructure.

India's 12th five year plan draft had been approved as of October 2012, but a final version was not yet publicly available. The draft 12th five year plan proposed to increase investment in higher education to 25% of all government education spending, as previously noted. This would result in growth of higher education spending from 1.12% of GDP to 1.5% – still falling far below China's expenditure on education in 2008 at 3.3% of GDP. Many Indians, however, are not waiting for the government to correct the current education shortfall, and rapid development of private colleges to satiate educational demand have contributed to strong growth in the numbers of higher education institutions over the past decade (Figure 2.4). It is of note that India's total number of higher education institutions is now the largest of any country in the world.

The Economist reports that a high level of private investment into education is ongoing: "Meanwhile private money is flooding into tertiary education. Several tycoons, rather than leaving their entire fortunes to their children, have endowed universities such as the OP Jindal University (named after a steel family), the Azim Premji University (after the founder of Wipro) and the Shiv Nadar University (after the founder of HCL). They are paying higher salaries for good faculty, luring Indian academics from foreign universities and encouraging research as well as teaching."[49] Unfortunately for Indian students, the quality of many other private educational institutions is lacking, and as previously noted, this has a serious effect on their employability in the workforce.

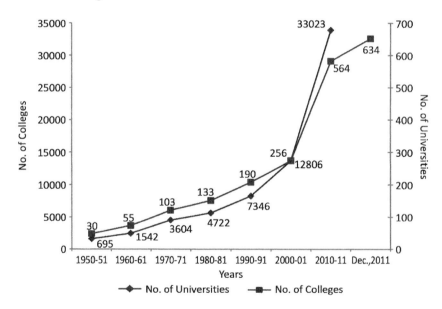

Figure 2.4: The Growth of Higher Education Institutions in India, 1950-2011[50]

As stated throughout the literature, when young Indian students consider educational choices, the role of the family is strong. Families do not typically respect and support Indian students who choose less technical fields such as the arts. Particularly in the case of male children, both family and society place pressure on young students to strive for a successful career with good salary prospects, and unlike in the U.S.,

> *"The hierarchy of an Indian classroom became clear – the bright kids would become engineers, the rich kids would become doctors, and the dumb kids would go into arts. Why? Because it wasn't difficult to get into arts school. It was always looked down upon if you came across someone with a B.A, even though he might be exceptionally bright and pursued arts for the love of it. The caste system, being abolished in Indian culture, had found its way into the Indian classroom in another form altogether – engineers, doctors and arts majors."*[51]

there is a strong expectation that children will follow the family's wishes. As an example, Dan Simon of CNN notes, "We also interviewed a highly trained engineer in San Francisco, Sandip Roy, who grew up in India. His parents expected him to become an engineer and he did just that, eventually earning a six-figure salary in Silicon Valley. But Roy wasn't personally fulfilled and desperately wanted to do something else. His biggest fear: disappointing his family."[52]

Self-sufficiency is also a key driver in the Indian family – 'standing on your own feet' is a commonly used phrase. In the *India Science Report* of 2005 the occupation of the head of the family was also found to influence the choice of the child, as well as parents and teachers playing a vital role in course and career choices for the children.[53] 'Choice' is perhaps an erroneous word to use here, as unlike in the U.S., where students choose the field they wish to study with respect to their desire, Indian students may often pick a field or have one picked for them irrespective of their desires. It was found to be a common thread in the literature and in personal interviews that Indian students often chose to study fields such as engineering and then later learned to enjoy it, rather than showing specific personal interest or aptitude in the field. Engineering was found in the *India Science Report* to be the preferred subject among children of salary earners and businessmen, the two highest earning categories, while for wage earners and agriculturalists (considered low salary earners), subjects such as the arts were preferred.[54] This was possibly because students either could not get into engineering colleges due to low scores and/or strong competition, or their families could not afford the cost of top tier institutions such as the IITs.

China

Chinese cultural attitudes towards science and engineering are more similar to those of India than those in the U.S. A 1998 survey examining the ties between Chinese culture and technological development makes reference to China's young students being directed toward science and

> *"I [former U.S. secretary of education William J. Bennett] just returned from a trip to Beijing, where I spoke with Chinese parents about the value of American education, where we excel and where we fall short. Not surprising was the extent to which the Chinese value education, especially primary and secondary education, and yearn for their children to attend American universities, and if possible, stay in America. When I engaged Chinese parents about their children, they would often say, 'My son (or daughter) is going to Princeton (or fill in the elite American university).' I would respond, 'Great! What year is your son or daughter right now?' And they would say, 'Three years old.' High standards and high expectations are the norm in China, not the exception, as is often the case in the United States."[55]*

engineering fields by their parents. "It is interesting to note that young Chinese from modern China have shown ... a strong desire for sending their offspring on scientific courses of studies."[56] This tendency is also explored in the following statistics from NSF's *Science and Engineering Indicators*, which notes that "Among Chinese, science (40%) ranked close to medicine (41%) and teaching (43%) as an occupation that survey respondents hoped their children would pursue."[57]

As early as 1963, China's Four Modernizations were proposed by the Premier of the time, Zhou Enlai – these were the fields of National Defense, Agriculture, Industry and Science and Technology, the latter being of particular note in this discussion. In 1978, Deng Xiaoping officially launched the Four Modernizations, with the hope that they would result in both the modernization of the People's Republic of China, and its elevation to self-reliant economic power. Thus, there is a national importance given to engineering, and Chinese culture dictates that serving society is of high importance.

Chinese government policy changes had a significant effect on engineering enrollment, directing greater numbers of students into universities over the past two decades. As Wadhwa et al. notes, the Chinese leadership had a number of reasons for such policies, including "long-term development needs for more domestically trained engineers, medium-term goals to help China upgrade by building a competitive position in knowledge-intensive industries, and short-term causes like the Asian financial crisis in the late 1990s and the ascension of Zhu Rongji to the position of Premier in 1998."[58] The authors also note that because the vast majority of universities were public organizations, central and provincial governments were able to successfully apply pressure to increase engineering enrollment numbers. Undergraduate engineering enrollment numbers in China have been very high, as illustrated in Figure 2.5.

In contrast with the U.S., in China emphasis on a rigorous and demanding education is part of the culture and a high level of performance in the educational system is seen as a requirement for future success. The structure of education is more rigid and focused on rote learning, memorization, and test score performance, primarily in preparation for the *gaokao*, or national university entrance exam, a multiple-day test of a high school education that millions of Chinese students face each year. In June 2012, 9 million Chinese students took the exam, with only 6.85 million university spots available.[59] Secondary school students in China also face an exam at the end of each school year to determine eligibility for the next year – if they fail, they cannot proceed to the next grade.[60]

China's 'one family, one child' policy also results in a more pronounced responsibility on the shoulders of the family's only child to work hard in school and be successful, as he or she alone represents the hopes and dreams of the family. All of the above pressures on Chinese students, many of which U.S. students do not face, result in a culture more keenly focused on meeting educational performance standards than that of the U.S.

There are problems, however, within China's educational system, and the country's education concerns can be primarily attributed to the *gaokao*. Evidently, even in 2012, "critics say the exam promotes the kind of rote learning that is endemic to education in China and that hobbles creativity."[61] *The Economist* reports that "the *gaokao* system ... promotes the survival of the fittest, but not of the best. The students are trained exclusively for the studying and answering of test papers. But the majority lack the skills to join in classroom discussion. Independence of thought is subordinated to the demands of rote learning. The students who emerge from this system often find it difficult to make basic social engagement, let alone intellectual collaboration."[62] While extraordinarily large numbers of students successfully make it through the Chinese educational system each year, and go on to further their education in Chinese and international universities, the system is in many cases struggling to adequately prepare such students to join the new global S&E workforce.

The Ministry of Science and Technology of the People's Republic of China regularly releases data on the status of science and engineering efforts in the form of the *China Science and Technology Statistic Data Book*, last published in 2007. The strong popularity of engineering in the country can be understood from an examination of Figure 2.3. The figure shows that S&E fields encompass 40% of all students who enroll and graduate, while about 7% go into medicine, and law represents only 5% of all students.

全国普通高等学校分学科学生数 (2005~2006)
National students in regular institutions of higher education by field of study

千人 1,000 persons

	2005		2006	
	毕业生 Graduates	在校学生 Enrolments	毕业生 Graduates	在校学生 Enrolments
大学生数 Undergraduates	3068.0	15617.8	3774.7	17388.4
理学 Science	164.9	967.9	197.2	1047.9
工学 Engineering	1091.0	5477.2	1341.7	6143.9
农学 Agriculture	69.5	308.1	77.2	331.6
医学 Medicine	202.6	1132.2	253.3	1268.6
管理学 Administration	506.2	2780.4	656.1	3233.4
哲学 Philosophy	1.3	6.3	1.4	6.8
经济学 Economics	163.0	857.8	204.0	921.4
法学 Law	163.5	697.2	186.2	710.2
教育学 Education	280.1	1022.7	322.3	1029.6
文学 Literature	415.2	2318.7	524.8	2642.4
历史学 History	10.7	49.4	10.6	52.5

Figure 2.5: Chinese Students in Regular Institutions of Higher Education by Field of Study[63]

When sorting the above data for 2006, it can be seen that engineering as both an enrollment choice and field of graduation is dominant in China – more than twice as popular as the 2nd and 3rd position fields combined, and it is clear that this dominance was the case in 2005 also.

Mu-ming Poo, a U.S.-based professor at the University of California, Berkeley, created the Institute of Neuroscience in China and was a past chair of the Department of Biological Sciences and Biotechnology at Tsinghua University. Poo noted that scientists are still respected as crucial elements of Chinese society, and as such, they have been given financial support from the Chinese government at unprecedented levels. Of current Chinese students, Poo says, "the brightest young people still go into science and technology rather than business and law school."[64]

The emphasis on technology at the highest levels in China is evident when we consider the response of Premier Wen Jiabao to an earthquake in China; he led the response with a level of technical authority that few politicians anywhere could match. The Tianjin native studied geological surveying as an undergraduate and geological structure as a graduate student at the Beijing Institute of Geology from 1960 to 1968, then spent the next 14 years with the Gansu Provincial Geological Bureau in Western China. An example of his keen interest in and understanding of science and technology is the following exchange, taken from "China's Scientist Premier":

> *"Question:* In the United States, we often talk about the fact that the real innovation, if we look backwards, comes from fundamental science, basic science, that was done 20 to 25 years earlier. When I visited the Ministry of Science and Technology, I was told that China's investment in what we call basic research has been fixed at 5% of total research investment. Do you think that is the right number?
>
> *Answer:* Personally, I attach great importance to research in fundamental sciences because I believe that no applied or developmental research can do without basic research as the wellspring and driving force. But, in this world of ours, often because of material gains and immediate interests, it is easy to neglect basic research. This should be avoided. In recent years, we have continuously increased the level of support but I think the [investment] ratio is still insufficient."[65]

As a further illustration of how heavily Chinese culture is invested in the importance of science and technology, the country's targeted spending on research and development is 2.5% of GDP by 2020 – it is currently 1.5% and climbing. The growth of R&D expenditures in China has been the most significant in the world over the past decade, with an average of greater than 19%, whereas in the U.S. growth has hovered between 2.6% and 2.8% annually for the same period.[66] Clearly, China is focused on trying to build itself into a science and technology powerhouse on the global stage.

Conclusion

Culture influences young students who study engineering and other

STEM fields. Unlike U.S. students, those in India and China choose their field of study and career based on societal and familial pressures to be self-sufficient and successful, not strictly on personal interest. These students spend more time in school, face more competition for college positions, and as a group expend greater overall time on academic pursuits than their counterparts in the U.S. Their cultures revere those who succeed in engineering in a way our country does not – particularly in China, where the majority of the country's leadership are engineers. In the U.S., beyond overall issues with the public's low level of understanding of the field of engineering and what engineers do, a range of specific issues is brought into play from minority cultures, who are seriously underrepresented in engineering. Engineering in the U.S. has an identity issue, as students deem the educational workload too difficult compared to other fields, as the system 'weeds out' those unprepared for it, as it breeds an unpopular 'geek' culture, and as it is not as inviting to minority groups and women as it could be. In terms of our educational system in the U.S – a crucial component to our future engineering success – we are not measuring up to the nations we now compete against. As one expert notes in the film *2 Million Minutes*, "America is the one country in the world that doesn't seem to recognize that it's in competition for the great minds and the capital of the world."[67] The fact that we fail to understand that engineers are crucial to meeting our future challenges[68] is indicative of a dangerous disconnect in U.S. culture – we simply do not understand and appreciate the criticality of engineering, not only to our daily lives, but to our future global competitiveness.

References

1. Petroski, H. (2009). *American Society for Engineering Education, Refractions, Polarizing Cultures: A 1959 warning about the arts-science divide deserves a new look.* Prism, October 2009, retrieved from <http://www.prism-magazine.org/oct09/refractions.cfm>
2. Ibid.
3. Frehill, L.M. (2004). *The Gendered Construction of the Engineering Profession in the United States, 1893-1920.* Men and Masculinities 6, no. 4, 383-403. And Oldenziel, R. (1999). *Making Technology Masculine: Women, Men, and the Machine in America, 1880-1945.* (Amsterdam: Amsterdam University Press).
4. Authors' analysis of 2009 American Community Survey weighted data indicated that only 4 percent of all engineers in the U.S. worked for themselves (either incorporated or unincorporated) compared to 10 percent of the entire U.S. workforce.

5. Hart Research Associates (2009). *Hart Research Associates; Memorandum: Americans Attitudes Toward Engineering and Engineering Challenges-National Survey Results*. Retrieved from <http://summit-grandchallenges.pratt.duke.edu/files/grandchallenges/Hart_survey_engineering.pdf>

6. There are various sets of countries/economies that have become the focus of international comparative research about economic development, broadly speaking, and issues associated with science and engineering as they relate to economic development. Brazil, Russian Federation, India and China are the "BRIC" group that is popular. Some analysts add South Africa to this grouping to look at the BRICS nations. A 2010 report on science and technology strategies in six nations added Japan and Singapore (and removed South Africa) from this list to use the acronym JBRICS.

7. For a review of the literature in this area, see Van de Werfhorst, H.G. and Mijs, J.J.B. (2010). *Achievement inequality and the institutional structure of educational systems: A comparative perspective.* Annual Review of Sociology, 36: 407-428.

8. Arulmani, G. (2009). *The Internationalization of Career Counseling: Bridging Cultural Processes and Labour Market Demands in India.* Asian Journal of Counseling, 16(2): 149-170.

9. Hart Research (2009). *Hart Research Associates; Memorandum: Americans' Attitudes Toward Engineering and Engineering Challenges-National Survey Results*. Retrieved from <http://summit-grand-challenges.pratt.duke.edu/files/grandchallenges/Hart_survey_engineering.pdf>

10. Arulmani, G. (2009). *The Internationalization of Career Counseling: Bridging Cultural Processes and Labour Market Demands in India.* Asian Journal of Counseling, 16(2): 149-170.

11. Berkelaar, B.L., et al. (2012). *'First, it's dirty. Second, it's dangerous. Third, it's insulting': Urban Chinese Children Talk about Dirty Work.* Communication Monographs, 79.1: 93-114.

12. Lowell, B.L., Salzman, H., Bernstein, H. with Henderson, E. (2009, November). Steady as She Goes? Three Generations of Students through the Science and Engineering Pipeline. In *Annual Meetings of the Association for Public Policy Analysis and Management Washington DC* on November (Vol 7., No. 2009, pp. 9-10).

13. One of the key differences in the U.S. is that there has been a historic belief in mathematics as an innate ability – so that poor performance has traditionally been "accepted" as "You're just not good at math." This is in direct contrast to the Asian (and Asian-American)

approach, which sees mathematics as any other skill that can be learned and improved via practice.

14. Loftus, M., (2006). A Future Engineer?. *ASEE Prism*, 16(2), 26-31.
15. Harris Interactive (2009, August). *The Harris Poll #86.*
16. Arulmani, G. (2009). The Internationalization of Career Counseling: Bridging Cultural Processes and Labour Market Demands in India. *Asian Journal of Counseling* 16(2): 149-170.
17. Lin, N., and Xie, W. (1988). Occupational prestige in urban China. *American Journal of Sociology*, 793-832.
18. Zakaria, F. (2011). *Restoring the American Dream: Fixing Education.* Fareed Zakaria GPS, CNN, Original Air Date November 12, 2011, retrieved from <http://transcripts.cnn.com/TRANSCRIPTS/1111/12/fzgps.01.html>
19. Lynn, L. and Salzman, H. (2010). The globalization of technology development: Implications for U.S. skills policy. *A US Skills System for the 21st Century: Innovations in Workforce Education and Development,* Finegold, D., M. Gatta, H. Salzman, S. Shurman (Eds.) LERA Research Volume.
20. Silobreaker.com/Wikipedia.com/India.gov.in, result of searches for "India", "India Cabinet Ministers" and individual member names both on these sites and on www.google.com and associated results pages.
21. Chinavitae.com and Wikipedia.com, result of searches for "China politburo" and individual member names both on these sites and on www.google.com and associated results pages.
22. Florman, S. C. (1994). *The Existential Pleasures of Engineering.* St. Martins, Griffin.
23. King, C.J., (2012). "Restructuring Engineering Education: Why, How and When?." *Journal of Engineering Education* 101, no. 1, 1-5.
24. Mervis, J. (2010). Better Intro Courses Seen as Key to Reducing Attrition of STEM Majors. *Science*, Vol 330, October 2010, p. 306.
25. Boundaoul, A. (2011). *Why would-be engineers end up as English majors*, CNN, May 2011, retrieved from <http://www.cnn.com/2011/US/05/17/education.stem.graduation/index.html>
26. Kantrowitz, M. (2011). *Student Aid Policy Analysis, The Distribution of Grants and Scholarships by Race.* September 2011, <http://www.finaid.org/scholarships/20110902racescholarships.pdf>
27. Frehill, L., DiFabio, N., and Hill, S. (2008). *Confronting the 'New' American Dilemma, Underrepresented Minorities in Engineering: A Data-Based Look at Diversity.* National Action Council for Minorities in Engineering, Inc., p. 4.

28. Plosky, E. J. (1999). *Understanding MIT's geek culture*. Retrieved from <http://www.subjectverb.com/www/writing/geekculture.html>

29. Harris Interactive (2004). *American Perspectives on Engineers and Engineering. Conducted for the American Association of Engineering Societies.* Retrieved from <http://www.aaes.org/harris_2004_files/frame.htm>

30. Frehill, L., DiFabio, N., and Hill, S. (2008). *Confronting the 'New' American Dilemma, Underrepresented Minorities in Engineering: A Data-Based Look at Diversity.* National Action Council for Minorities in Engineering, Inc.

31. Crotty, J.M. (2011). Are Hispanics America's Next Great STEM Innovators? *Forbes*, retrieved from < http://www.forbes.com/sites/jamesmarshallcrotty/2011/11/22/are-hispanics-americas-next-great-stem-innovators/>

32. National Science Foundation (2012). *Women, Minorities, and Persons with Disabilities in Science and Engineering.* (NSB 11-309, Arlington, VA.) Table 2-1, retrieved from <http://www.nsf.gov/statistics/wmpd/pdf/tab2-1.pdf>.

33. Ibid, Table 2-10.

34. National Center for Children in Poverty (2012). Retrieved from <http://www.nccp.org/topics/childpoverty.html>

35. Macartney, S. (2011). *Child Poverty in the United States 2009 and 2010: Selected Race Groups and Hispanic Origin*, American Community Survey Briefs, United States Census Bureau, November 2011.

36. Beegle, D.M. (2003). Overcoming the Silence of Generational Poverty. *Talking Points*, October/November 2003. Retrieved from <http://www.combarriers.com/pdf/TP0151Overcoming.pdf>

37. Tang, M., "Psychological Effects on being Perceived as a 'Model Minority for Asian Americans." Chinese American Educational Research & Development Association, retrieved from <http://www.caerda.org/journal/index.php/newwaves/article/viewFile/11/9>

38. Steinberg, L., Dornbusch, S.M., and Brown, B.B. (1992) Ethnic differences in adolescent achievement. *American Psychologist*, 47, 1992, pp. 723-729.

39. Chubin, D.E., May, G.S., and Babco, E.L. (2005). Diversifying the Engineering Workforce. *Journal of Engineering Education*, 94(1), 73-86.

40. Frehill, L.M. (2012). Gender and Career Outcomes of U.S. Engineers. *International Journal of Gender, Science and Technology* 4(2), 148-166. Also Frehill, L.M. (2009). SWE Retention study and work/life balance, *SWE Magazine*, Fall 2009, 34-40.

41. Ruparel, H. (2011, May). *Why there are so many engineers in India.* The Next Web, retrieved from <http://thenextweb.com/in/2011/05/08/why-there-so-many-engineers-in-india/>

42. Banerjeee, R. and Muley, V.P. (2008). *Engineering education in India.* India Institute of Technology Bombay. Retrieved from <http://casi.sas.upenn.edu/system/files/Engineering+Education+in+India+Dec1608-1.pdf>

43. Battelle (2011). *2012 Global R&D Funding Forecast.* Retrieved from <http://battelle.org/docs/default-document-library/2012_global_forecast.pdf?sfvrsn=2>

44. Mathews, N. (2012). India boosts infrastructure budget but wants more private funds. *Engineering News-Record*, 268 (14).

45. The Economist (2012). *A Billion Brains*, September 2012.

46. Ibid.

47. Ibid.

48. Planning Commission, Government of India (2012). *Eleventh Five Year Plan (2007-2012),* retrieved from http://planningcommission.nic.in/plans/planrel/11thf.htm

49. The Economist (2012). *A Billion Brains*, September 2012.

50. University Grants Commission, India (2012). *Higher Education in India at a Glance.* Retrieved from <http://oldwebsite.ugc.ac.in/pub/HEglance2012.pdf>

51. Ruparel, H. (2011). *Why there are so many engineers in India.* The Next Web. Retrieved from <http://thenextweb.com/in/2011/05/08/why-there-so-many-engineers-in-india/>

52. Simon, D. (2007). *Asian-American kids feel career pressure*, Anderson Cooper 360 Blog, CNN, 16 May 2007, retrieved from <http://www.cnn.com/CNN/Programs/anderson.cooper.360/blog/2007/05/asian-american-kids-feel-career.html>

53. Shukla, R. (2005). *India Science Report, Science education, human resources and public attitude towards science and technology.* National Council of Applied Economic Research.

54. Ibid, Figure 2.7, page 16.

55. Bennett, W.J. (2012). Why the Chinese are flocking to U.S. colleges, *CNN*, May 31, 2012, retrieved from <http://www.cnn.com/2012/05/31/opinion/bennett-china-us-schools/index.html>

56. Chang, Z.Y. and Lee, K.B. (1998). Cultural aspect and technological development: a Chinese perspective. *Technovation*, Vol. 18, Issue 12, pp. 765-770.

57. National Science Foundation (2010). *Science and Engineering Indicators 2010*. Arlington, VA (NSB 10-01), pp. 7-36.

58. Wadhwa, V., Gereffi, G., Rissing, B., and Ong, R. (2008). Getting the numbers right: International Engineering Education in the United States, China and India. *Journal of Engineering Education*, 97(1), pp. 13-25.

59. MSNBC (2012). *A day of anxious waiting for parents in China as students take college entrance exams*. Retrieved from < http://photoblog.msnbc.msn.com/_news/2012/06/08/12121075-a-day-of-anxious-waiting-for-parents-in-china-as-students-take-college-entrance-exams>

60. University of Michigan (2012). *Synopsis of Chinese School System*, retrieved from <http://sitemaker.umich.edu/vanschaack.356/synopsis_of_public_sch ools_in_china>

61. Wong, E. (2012). Test That Can Determine the Course of Life in China Gets a Closer Examination. *The New York Times*, June 2012, retrieved from <http://www.nytimes.com/2012/07/01/world/asia/burden-of-chinas-college-entrance-test-sets-off-widedebate.html?_r=1&page wanted =all>

62. The Economist (2012). *Testing Times*. June 13th, 2012, retrieved from <http://www.economist.com/blogs/analects/2012/06/university-entrance-exams>

63. Ministry of Science and Technology of the People's Republic of China (2007). *China Science and Technology Statistics Data Book*. p.24, Table 3-4.

64. Wells, W.A. (2007). The Returning Tide: How China, the world's most populous country, is building a competitive research base. *Journal of Cell Biology*, 176(4), p. 380.

65. Xin, H. and Stone, R. (2008). China's Scientist Premier. *Science*, Vol. 322, p. 363.

66. National Science Foundation (2010). *Science and Engineering Indicators 2010*, Arlington, VA (NSB 10-01), pp. 4-5.

67. Compton, R.A., Raney, A., and Heeter, C. (2008). *Two Million Minutes: A Global Examination*. Broken Pencil Productions, Documentary Film, 54 Minutes.

68. Hart Research Associates (2009). *Americans' Attitudes Toward Engineering and Engineering Challenges-National Survey Results*. February 27th. Retrieved from <http://summit-grandchallenges.pratt.duke.edu/files/grandchallenges/Hart_survey_e ngineering.pdf>

Chapter 3

Immigration

"The revenue generated by Fortune 500 companies founded by immigrants or children of immigrants is greater than the GDP of every country in the world outside the U.S., except China and Japan. Seven of the 10 most valuable brands in the world come from American companies founded by immigrants or children of immigrants."[1]

The United States is 'a country of immigrants,' and these immigrants have played an important and significant role in the growth and vitality of our economy. Of particular interest in our study is the sub category of immigrants who have or are seeking S&T careers, and more specifically in the field of engineering. We will evaluate the historical levels of engineers migrating to the U.S., examine immigration policy issues both here and abroad, and consider the science and engineering accomplishments of immigrants and their children.

There is a general lack of comprehensive data on immigration for the period of interest from the INS (later known as USCIS) and other appropriate sources, such as Census data, the State Department, and the DOL, on immigration for the period of interest. Much of the available data either generalizes categories, omits categories such as profession, visa type or education, or is inconsistent over time. Also, NSF found that "there is insufficient detail, particularly to distinguish between new permanent residents, existing permanent immigrants, non-immigrants, and illegal residents."[2] Further, the definition of "scientist" or "engineer" as used in the INS data does not necessarily correspond with that NSF uses in its surveys of S&Es in the United States. A 2004 DHS Office of

Immigration Statistics report[3] listed "engineers" as a category under occupation, at 10,900, or 15% of the LPR category for 2004. However, in the same report for 2005 and subsequent years, these numbers do not reappear, and occupation categories are not broken down into the same categories. For example, NSF's 2008 *"Science and Engineering Indicators"* shows that 50% of immigrants were listed as skill type "unknown."

In spite of the shortcomings mentioned here, the NSF has collected and reported on some relevant historical data as part of its efforts to understand the issues facing S&Es in the U.S. This information, coupled with NSF's *Science and Engineering Indicators* for 2002, allowed us to generate Figure 3.1 for the 1968-1998 time period, illustrating the count of permanent visas issued in the S&E category. Information for 1999 and beyond S&E immigrant visas could not be located. It is not clear if the INS/USCIS stopped reporting these data or NSF stopped analyzing it, as these data do not appear on later NSF "Science and Engineering Indicators" reports, and are not seen in public INS/USCIS immigration statistical tables or reports. Numbers of S&Es from Figure 3.1 for the 27-year period that data were available (1968-1998) showed an average of 12,535 S&E permanent visas per year, with a total of 351,000 permanent visas issued.

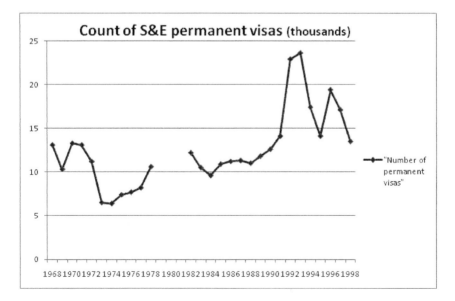

Figure 3.1: S&E Permanent Visas 1968 to 1998
(Data Unavailable for 1979 to 1981)[4]

The data on permanent visas show general stability from the 1968 to 1991 timeframe. The period of significant change thereafter is a result of two governmental policy changes. The first is a prediction by NSF in the late 1980s of a 675,000 shortfall of S&E workers, prompting significant immigration reform in the form of the 1990 Immigration and Naturalization Act (INA), which went into effect in late 1991. The INA's changes in immigration policy resulted in a 62% increase in the number of immigrant S&Es in 1992, and the slight additional increase in the number for 1993 was a result of the previous year's Chinese Student Protection Act (CSPA). This enabled Chinese nationals in the United States on student or other temporary visas to acquire permanent resident visas, resulting in 1,403 extra S&E immigrants for the year.[5]

Immigrant S&E counts began to revert back to previous levels as a result of fewer students naturalizing under the CSPA (down 17%) and the economic slowdown at the time, resulting in a perceived 'glut' of S&Es in the workforce in 1995. A popular study that year by RAND Corp. and Stanford's Institute for Higher Education Research indicated an over-supply – some 25% to 50% more than the economy at the time could absorb.[6] Significant technical problems were later reported with this study. Subsequently, NSF's 1996 count of permanent visas showed a 27% increase, in agreement with those who discounted the study's findings. Finally, 1997 and 1998 data showed a decline back to average numbers. Other information such as level of education was not available for S&Es in NSF's 1993 report,[7] and these historical data were not found to be analyzed elsewhere. Entry status information broken down by individual S&E categories was also not available for analysis.

The H-1B Skilled Worker Visa

The 1990 Immigration and Naturalization Act introduced the H-1B visa, a category that allows companies to bring in skilled workers (those with a bachelor's degree or equivalent who have theoretical or technical expertise in a specialized field) for a period of no more than six years, comprised of 2 three-year periods. At the end of this period, immigrant workers either return home, switch to another visa category, or become naturalized citizens. The importance of H-1B category in this discussion is that it is seen as a pipeline to allow skilled S&Es into the U.S. to replenish the supply depleted by both lower numbers of talented S&E graduates and the aging workforce – and if the cap were raised for high-skilled S&Es in particular, it is believed this could help to resolve shortages.

The available numbers or 'cap' for this class of visa is shown in Table 3.1. The cap began at 65,000 per year in 1990; in 1997 it was

revised to 115,000 for 1998 – 1999, after the cap was hit very quickly in
1997; then it went as high as 195,000 for three years, returning to 65,000
in FY2004 due to national security concerns. The cap remains low even
in FY2013, at the original count of 65,000. The H-1B Visa Reform Act
of 2004 added an additional 20,000 to this cap for any foreign workers
who held a Masters or higher level degree from a U.S. educational
institution.

Time Period	H-1B Visa Cap
FY 1990-1998	65,000
FY 1999-2000	115,000
FY 2001	Initially 107,500, then 195,000
FY 2002	195,000
FY 2003	195,000
FY 2004 to FY 2013	65,000 + 20,000

Table 3.1: H-1B Visa Caps by Year[8]

Demand exceeds the visa supply extraordinarily quickly each year,
as U.S. companies look for international talent (in S&E and other areas),
and as huge numbers of international workers look for positions within
the U.S. and flood the system with visa requests. As an indication of
pent-up international demand for skilled worker positions in the U.S.,
Table 3.2 shows the time periods for H-1B caps to be overrun from fiscal
year 2004-2013 (fiscal year begins October 1, applications accepted
April 1).

FY 2004 reached by February 2004 (with 7 months remaining in the fiscal year)
FY 2005-09 reached before Day 1 of the fiscal year.
FY 2010 - reached by December 21, 2009 (9 months remaining)
FY 2011 - reached by January 26, 2011 (8 months remaining)
FY 2012 - reached by November 22, 2011 (10 months remaining)
FY 2013 - reached by June 11, 2012 (3 1/2 months remaining)

Table 3.2: Time to Exceed H-1B Caps[9]

The DoD currently has a small exemption from the H-1B quota for
"up to 100 persons who will be performing services of an exceptional

nature in connection with Department of Defense (DoD) research and development projects or coproduction projects."[10] This falls under the H-1B2 category, but it is extraordinarily restrictive in its terms. The requirement for any position is that "the cooperative research and development project or a co-production project is provided for under a government-to-government agreement administered by the U.S. Department of Defense."[11] It is envisioned that this could expand in scope to become an additional area of exemption from the cap (in the same vein as the exemptions provided for educational institutions) to solve this issue over the short term; this expansion would occur along with a streamlined process to put immigrants into positions as soon as possible.

The H-1B visa application and approval process is quite slow and difficult for both the employer and the worker, and the expense is high. Streamlining it and adding requirements specific to the workforce needs would seem appropriate – i.e. a talented S&E worker is processed in half the time, is able to naturalize faster, but is required as part of the visa's conditions to work for a DoD lab for a certain period of time. For enlisting immigrant soldiers in the Armed Forces, Congress passed statutes in both 2003 and 2006 reducing restrictions. A cooperative effort between the military and the USCIS enabled expedited procedures for processing paperwork and biometrics for soldiers, reducing the need in many cases for legal permanent resident (LPR) or citizenship status when enlisting. Also, other measures intended to quickly naturalize those considered "vital to the national interest" were put in place.[12]

Many other technology companies and individuals have petitioned the government and its various agencies for many years to increase H-1B numbers, particularly those in the upper echelons of the S&T community. For example, Microsoft Chairman Bill Gates has spoken before Congress urging significant immigration reform. He asked Congress and the White House to extend the period that foreign students can work in the U.S. after graduation, raising the cap on H-1B visas, creating a clear path to permanent residency for highly-skilled foreign-born employees, and increasing the number of green cards. Gates noted, "To address the shortage of scientists and engineers, we must ... reform our education system and our immigration policies. If we don't, American companies simply will not have the talent they need to innovate and compete. ...The shortage of scientists and engineers is so acute that we must do both: reform our education system and reform our immigration policies. Without leadership from Congress and the president ... and the commitment of the private sector to do its part, the center of progress will shift to other nations that are more committed to the pursuit of innovation."[13]

President Obama has also spoken in support of an increase in H-1B numbers and longer-term immigration reform: "I will support a temporary increase in the H-1B visa program as a stopgap measure until we can reform our immigration system comprehensively. I support comprehensive immigration reform that includes improvement in our visa programs, including our legal permanent resident visa programs and temporary programs including the H-1B program, to attract some of the world's most talented people to America."[14] There are, however, those who oppose immigration reform for reasons of perceived threats to national security, pride in homegrown talent, and a belief that increases in programs such as H-1B would result in a smaller pool of positions being available for U.S. citizens. As a result, a number of bills that attempted to address immigration reform have never made it through the legislative process, including the SKIL Act of 2007, otherwise known as S. 1348: Comprehensive Immigration Reform Act of 2007. This Act included the following sections of interest:

- Exempts from the annual H-1B cap professionals who have earned advanced degrees (e.g. Master's degree or higher) from accredited United States universities and those who have been awarded a medical specialty certification based on post-doctoral training and experience in the United States.

- Raises the H-1B (specialty occupation) cap from 65,000 to 115,000 and creates a flexible system that adjusts with the market.

- Raises the immigrant visa (i.e., green card) cap from 140,000 to 290,000 and allows unused visas to fall forward annually.

- Retains current green card allocation so that majority of visas (57%) are reserved for highly-educated/skilled workers.

- Requires the creation of a pre-certification program that streamlines the adjudication process, and reduces paperwork burdens, for employers with a track record of compliance and who file multiple applications.[15]

The SKIL Act, had it passed, would have had a significant impact on immigration reform, and certainly would have gone a long way to resolve shortages of S&E talent.

In a report accompanying S. 3254, the National Defense Authorization Act (NDAA) for Fiscal Year 2013, Senate Committee on Armed Services notes the following: "The committee recommends a provision that would express a sense of Congress that would strongly urge the Department of Defense to investigate innovative mechanisms to access the pool of talent of non-United States citizens with advanced scientific and technical degrees from United States institutions of higher learning."[16] The committee additionally noted that the FY2012 NDAA contained a provision directing the Secretary of Defense to assess mechanisms both currently and potentially available to the DoD to "employ non-United States citizens with critical scientific and technical skills that are vital to the national security interests of the United States," with a report due to the committee by the end of 2012.

A March 2009 survey of 1,203 immigrants who had returned to their home countries mentioned H-1B visa issues, stating that a significant backlog of visa requests was building up with "tens of thousands of capable foreign undergraduate students and graduate students seeking ways to stay in the United States that are not as restrictive as the H-1B program."[17] The report noted that in order to try to stop this outflow of workers back to their home countries and retain talent, the U.S. may need to look at even more than just allowing greater numbers in the country – family-based immigration programs may also be a part of an effective solution. Table 3.3 shows the U.S. in last place out of the ten countries listed in terms of the percentage of incoming immigrants migrating under work-based visas, reflecting the level of restrictions in place in U.S. immigration policy compared to other countries.

Country	Total Number (thousands)	Work (%)	Family (%)	Humanitarian (%)	Other (%)
South Korea	195	81	17	0	2
Switzerland	139	80	14	5	2
Spain	392	79	20	0	1
Italy	425	65	31	3	1
Germany	228	59	22	16	2
U.K.	347	58	31	1	10
Australia	206	42	51	6	1
France	168	34	52	7	8
Canada	247	25	62	13	0
U.S.	1107	7	73	15	5

Table 3.3: Share of Work-based Immigrants[18]

The visa process is a major bottleneck in providing additional skilled foreign nationals to supplement our domestic supply of scientists and engineers. Anderson notes in a National Foundation for American Policy brief that a skilled Indian citizen sponsored in 2011 for an EB-3 work-based immigrant visa may potentially wait up to 70 years for a green card, because only approximately 2,800 Indian professionals are granted permanent residence status each year under this category. He lists the backlog of Indian applicants for this category in 2011 at 210,000.[19] Further wait times for this category are seen in Table 3.5.

Country	Visas Issued
India	72,438
China-mainland	10,849
U.K.	3,660
South Korea	3,501
Mexico	2,647
Philippines	2,369
France	2,069
Japan	2,054
China-Taiwan	1,705
Germany	1,627
Other	26,215
Total	129,134

Table 3.4: H-1B Visas Issued by Nationality, FY 2011[20]

Such a backlog is created by per-country limits on employment-based immigration. In a legislative attempt to begin to remedy this issue, H.R. 3012, or the "Fairness for High-Skilled Immigrants Act of 2011," has passed the House of Representatives and awaits a vote in Congress. It would amend the Immigration and Nationality Act to both eliminate the current per-country limitation for employment-based visas, and increase family-sponsored immigration allowances.[21] Similar legislation has been put forth in the 'Startup Act 2.0', introduced on May 22, 2012 by U.S. Senators Marco Rubio (R-Fla.), Chris Coons (D-Del.), Jerry Moran (R-Kan.) and Mark Warner (D-Va.).[22] The Act aims to revise immigration law to allow foreign students who receive a Masters or Ph.D. in STEM fields at U.S. universities to receive a green card upon graduation. It also would eliminate the per-country cap on employment-based immigrant visas and create an "entrepreneur visa" for legal immigrants who start a business employing U.S. workers.[23]

	India (Persons with Priority Dates between July 8 2002 and July 15, 2004)	India (Persons with Priority Dates between July 15, 2004 and Nov. 22, 2005)	India (Persons with Priority Dates after Nov. 22, 2005 up to the present)	China (Persons with Priority Dates between July 15, 2004 and Nov. 22, 2005)	China (Persons with Priority Dates after Nov. 22, 2005 up to the present)	All Other Countries (Persons with Priority Dates after Nov. 22, 2005 up to the present)
How Long Have Most Been Waiting So Far (up to today)?	7 to 9 years	6 to 7 years	1 to 6 years	6 to 7 years	1 to 6 years	1 to 6 years
How Much Longer to Wait If No Change in Policy?	Up to another 11 years	Up to another 12 to 20 years	Another 21 to 70 years	2 to 3 years	4 to 24 years	1 to 5 years

Table 3.5: Projected Wait Times for Employment-based Green Cards (Third Preference, EB-3)[24]

Student Visas

While the F-1 student visa category allows hundreds of thousands of international students each year to come to the U.S. to pursue undergraduate and graduate degrees in S&E, the path beyond their education is less clear. International student enrollment in engineering programs at higher education institutions in the U.S. was at 135,592 in 2011, representing 18.7% of international students across all fields and an increase of 6.4% from 2009/2010 totals.[25] With engineering representing more than double the number of international students from any other S&E discipline and second only to business (21.5%), it is not surprising that the populous countries of India and China represent the home country of almost half of these students.

So what happens to these international engineering students when they graduate? It turns out many may return home, using their U.S.-gained talents to work for companies or start their own companies to compete against the U.S. on the global stage. As Peggy Blumenthal, Chief Operating Officer of the Institute of International Education, notes, "the growing economies of India and China provide strong employment opportunities for students trained in the U.S. in these two fields ... so they will see an immediate return on their investment in a U.S. degree."[26]

The F-1 student visa allows 60 days after conclusion of studies to prepare for departure from the U.S., transfer to another school or apply for Optional Practical Training (OPT), a one year option that allows students to work in the U.S. before again changing status or returning home. For those with degrees in STEM fields, this initial one year period may be extended by 17 months, allowing for 29 months in total in the U.S. before either an application must be filed for an employer-sponsored H-1B visa, or the student must return home. However, while the H-1B allows for up to 6 years of employment, it does not necessarily lead to a green card and permanent resident status. Applying for a green card (or LPR) is an additional process that depends on further employer effort and expenditure, and it often takes many years. Additionally, in some cases the H-1B visa may not be extended, depending upon the applicant's green card application status. In those cases the applicant would be required to return to his or her home country. Compared to other countries, the U.S. has a very difficult, expensive and time consuming visa process, and it has the disadvantage of possibly requiring the applicant to return home at multiple points throughout the process. New York mayor Michael Bloomberg summed up this issue in late 2009, saying that "we're committing what I call national suicide ... somehow or other, after 9/11 we went from reaching out and trying to get the best and the brightest to come here, to trying to keep them out. In fact, we do the stupidest thing, we give them educations and then don't give them green cards."[27]

Global Competition

While the U.S. turns away some international students after a period of time for visa policy reasons, other countries are beginning to compete for students and S&E professionals, and their visa policies may be more attractive to both students and skilled immigrants. *Beyond 'Fortress America'*, a National Academy of Sciences report, noted back in 2009 that "universities around the world now have the research equipment and infrastructure to compete with their American counterparts ... foreign universities are well positioned to extend competing offers."[28] Many countries have established national policies over the past decade to increase international enrollments, with positive effects. France's enrollments grew by 80% from 2000 to 2006, Australia's grew by 75%, Japan's grew by 95% (with policy in place to grow by 300% by 2020), and China's grew by 500% from 1997-2008 to 190,000 students, with a goal of 500,000 by 2020.[29] The NSF noted that while the U.S. remains the primary destination for both undergraduate and graduate international students, our share of global international students decreased from 24% in 2000 to 19% in 2008.[30] It is clear we cannot simply assume international students will continue to choose to be educated in the U.S. in the same numbers as in past decades.

Due to their domestic needs for scientists and engineers and other skilled workers, other countries are also more aggressively competing with the U.S for talented S&E workers. In Australia, a recent review noted that the country is particularly dependent on migrant engineers, stating that "Engineering is far more dependent on skilled migration than is the case for non-engineering skills. In 2010, the overseas born share of employment was 52.6% in engineering compared to 36.0% for non-engineering skills and 26.8% for the general labour force."[31] Australia's immigration policies reflect the country's desire for higher skilled workers, and those policies also include a skilled occupations list updated regularly to reflect labor needs, and a customized "SkillSelect" program that offers visa preference to those applicants who best fit current industry needs. The country also offers a temporary visa for skilled graduates, allowing international students 18 months to build the skills and job sponsorship needed for a permanent skilled visa.[32]

> *"We think of ourselves as the world's great immigrant society, and of course, for most of the country's history, that has been true. But something fascinating has happened over the past two decades. Other countries have been transforming themselves into immigrant societies, adopting many of America's best ideas and even improving on them. The result: the U.S. is not as exceptional as it once was, and its immigration advantage is lessening."[33]*

Some other examples of preferable immigration policy include New Zealand's work-to-residence visa, where a permanent visa can be applied for after 2 years. The country has also made a large investment in significantly expediting student visa processing times. Israel has developed a job placement program, held its first conference designed to connect Ph.D.-level S&E's with employers within the country, and launched its I-CORE program, designed to draw up to 2,400 Israeli scientists back to Israel. Canada implemented new immigration laws to allow prioritization of applications for those with needed skills, as well as provide visas for workers to address regional areas of need. Canada has also encouraged students to stay in the country, with a 3 year work visa provided even without a job offer in hand, and a permanent visa for up to 1,000 students who have completed two years of a Ph.D. in a STEM field.[34]

To bolster its domestic institutions, China has developed competitive policies for recalling S&E migrants who have moved abroad. China's National Medium and Long Term Development Plan attempts to lure back Chinese-born STEM workers from abroad who hold patents, or are prominent professors, or are recently graduated Ph.D. students. The country's Thousand Talents Plan looks to recruit 2,000 scientific elites and other experts from the U.S. So far, of the people listed as having been successfully recruited by the program, 55% have come from the U.S. In the Young Thousand Talents program, 77% have come from the U.S. The country also uses some aggressive lures to bring in scientific talent from abroad, including signing bonuses (up to US$158,000), free housing, tax breaks, prestigious titles, access to business incubators, and residency in major cities in China.[35]

Table 3.6 illustrates the many changes and improvements made by other countries in their immigration policy and procedures in an effort to not only attract the best and brightest from the U.S. and other countries, but to regain them once they have migrated away. Clearly, U.S.

immigration policy must change to face the new reality that we are now in serious competition with the world for talented S&Es.

Immigrant Advancement

Immigration of 'high-skilled' scientists and engineers has led to great benefits for the upper echelons of science and engineering fields, as illustrated in the following analyses of foreign-born members of two leading worldwide engineering societies. The grade of "Fellow," bestowed by the American Society of Mechanical Engineers (ASME), is given in recognition of the exceptional talents of society's brightest mechanical engineers. An engineer becomes a Fellow of ASME by being nominated by fellow members, thereby ensuring only the highest quality nominations. We reviewed this membership group to gauge the impact of foreign born S&Es. For the purposes of this analysis the term 'foreign born' was defined as individuals who were currently working in the U.S., and where evidence was present that either that they were born in another country or earned their undergraduate degree from an institution outside the U.S. The determination of foreign-born or not was made based on analysis of a number of data sources, including Google searches, biographies, curriculum vitae, or any other relevant material.

Country	Prioritize economic needs	Lure highly educated labor	Focus policies on sectors	Focus policies on religions	Streamline immigration process	Integrate immigrants into society	Tap international students	Visa for immigrant entrepreneurs	Adapt to changing conditions	Recruit expatriate talent
Australia	X	X	X	X	X	X	X	X	X	
Canada	X	X	X	X	X	X	X	X	X	
Chile					X			X		
China	X	X					X	X		X
Germany	X	X	X		X	X	X	X	X	
Ireland	X	X			X	X	X	X	X	X
Israel		X			X	X				X
Singapore	X	X	X		X	X	X	X	X	
U.K.	X	X	X				X	X	X	
U.S.		X						X		

Table 3.6: Summary of Immigration Policies by Country[36]

The origin of ASME members who have been elevated to Fellow status from 2004 to 2009 is shown in Table 3.8. We note that foreign-born fellows comprised 42% of all fellows working in the U.S., or 209 out of the total of 503, a very significant contribution to the makeup of the ASME Fellow grade. Further analysis of the numbers shows that 30% of the 209 high achievers originate from India, 15% from China, and another 15% from Taiwan (See Table 3.7). Clearly, India has had great success in exporting its talent to the U.S. to have such high numbers as part of an elite group of engineers.

Total ASME members elevated to Fellow status 2004-2009	627	
Total working in U.S.	503	80% of combined 2004-09 overall totals
Total foreign-born in U.S.	209	42% of total Fellows working in the U.S.
Top 5 countries of Origin : 2004-09		**(% of all foreign-born members 2004-2009)**
India	62	30%
China	31	15%
Taiwan	31	15%
UK	12	6%
Turkey	9	4%

(Source: Author's analysis of various online data from IEEE, ASME, Google, University websites and other relevant sources)

Table 3.7: ASME Fellows 2004-2009 – Background Analysis

Further examination of newly added ASME fellows from 2010-2011 also found that 63 out of the 137 new Fellows were foreign born, or 46%, reflecting the continuing trend of strong foreign-born representation within ASME.[37] Interestingly, in 2012 eight of the eleven highly honored ASME members receiving a medal for meritorious contributions to the field were foreign born engineers.

Institute of Electrical and Electronics Engineers (IEEE) 'Fellow' status follows a similar pattern as that of ASME. The IEEE Fellow grade is much the same as that of ASME, being based upon exceptional performance in IEEE-related fields. It was established in 1912 by one of the two original organizations that merged to later form IEEE, and is recognized worldwide as a badge of particular distinction for engineering professionals. As such, it is also a good barometer with which to gauge the impact of foreign-born S&E professionals into the upper levels of professional recognition in the U.S. Entries such as "Canada/Greece" refer to the countries having the same number, not a combined number. Of the 589 total new IEEE Fellow status holders in 2008-09, 360 were found to be working in the U.S., and as such those are the Fellows on which further analysis was focused. Table 3.9 clearly shows again a significant percentage of these individuals being foreign-born in both 2008 (34%) and 2009 (39%). India again is the most common country of origin, with an average of 26% of the 2008-09 foreign-born Fellows; however, China is not far behind at an average of 21.5% over the two years. This data also indicates that the Chinese are more interested in electrical engineering, which is a more rapidly growing industry in China, both for electronic manufacturing in general and computers in particular.

ASME Fellows	Total in U.S.	Working Outside U.S.	U.S. Origin	U.S. %	Foreign Born Total	Foreign Born %
2009	70	26	35	50%	35	50%
2008	49	11	31	63%	18	37%
2007	97	20	63	65%	34	35%
2006	105	26	54	51%	51	49%
2005	105	26	65	62%	40	38%
2004	77	15	46	60%	31	40%

(Source: Author's analysis of various online data from IEEE, ASME, Google, University websites and other relevant sources)

Table 3.8: ASME Fellows 2004-2009

The presence and impact of immigrants into the upper levels of the science and engineering fields is impressive. Senior faculty members of the Mechanical Engineering departments of the top 10 highest ranked U.S. universities, according to the 2010 *U.S. News and World Report*[38] and the University of Maryland (the home University of the authors) is shown in Table 3.10.

Information for these faculty members in most cases was readily available on the individual university websites of each Mechanical Engineering department. Foreign-born is defined again as individuals who are currently working in the U.S., with either evidence found that they were born in another country, or with an undergraduate degree listed as being from an institution outside the U.S.

Total IEEE members elevated to Fellow status 2008-09	589	
Total working in U.S.	360	61% of combined 2008-09 overall totals
Total foreign-born in U.S.	131	36% of total Fellows working in the U.S.
2008 foreign-born	66	34% of 2008 total Fellows working in U.S.
2009 foreign-born	65	39% of 2009 total Fellows working in US
Top 5 countries of origin - 2008		**(% of the 66 foreign-born Fellows working in the U.S.)**
India	16	24%
China	12	18%
Taiwan	5	8%
Russia	4	6%
Germany	3	5%
Top 5 countries of origin - 2009		**(% of the 65 total foreign-born fellows working in the U.S.)**
India	18	28%
China	10	15%
Canada/Greece	4	6%
Israel/Pakistan/Turkey	3	5%
Belgium/Italy/South Korea/Taiwan	2	3%

(Source: Author's analysis of various online data from IEEE, ASME, Google, University websites and other relevant sources)

Table 3.9: IEEE Fellows 2008-09 – Background Analysis

An examination of the above results shows once again a strong presence of foreign-born individuals at these institutions – across the 11 Mechanical Engineering colleges, they comprise an average 46.5% of the faculty. At 7 of the universities, faculty members of Indian origin were the highest percentage, leading to a total percentage of 20% of foreign-born faculty over the 10 locations. China again takes second place, at 13% overall. It is an interesting juxtaposition that India and China, considered two major competitors to the U.S. in terms of buildup of S&E personnel resources, are also the countries of origin for a surprising number of not only the faculty at the top ten Mechanical Engineering colleges in the U.S., but also two top engineering associations.

University	Total M.E. Faculty	Of U.S. Origin	U.S. Origin %	Foreign Born Total	Foreign Born %
MIT	87	51	59%	36	41%
Stanford	36	20	56%	16	44%
UC Berkeley	41	21	51%	20	49%
Cal Tech	19	10	53%	9	47%
U Michigan Ann Arbor	66	28	42%	38	58%
Georgia Tech	93	49	53%	44	47%
U Illinois – Urbana Champaign	51	20	39%	31	61%
Purdue – West Lafayette	67	35	52%	32	48%
Cornell	45	31	69%	14	31%
Princeton	23	14	61%	9	39%
University of Maryland	48	24	50%	24	50%

(Source: Author's analysis of various online data from IEEE, ASME, Google, University websites and other relevant sources)

Table 3.10: Faculty in Mechanical Engineering Departments

The National Center for Education Statistics (NCES), as part of its *2004 National Study of Postsecondary Faculty* report, also allows for an analysis of the background of faculty members at all U.S. colleges and universities. Across all research fields the percentage of foreign-born faculty is listed at 15.5%; however, the field that foreign-born faculty gravitate towards when working in the U.S. can be clearly seen – engineering is listed as 45.4% foreign-born, almost 50% higher than the next closest field, natural sciences.

Besides engineering faculty, many of the nation's other top science and engineering establishments are clearly comprised of a large number of immigrants – as further noted by Fallows in *The Atlantic*: "'My favorite statistic is that one-quarter of the members of the National Academy of Sciences were born abroad,' I was told by Harold Varmus, the president of the Memorial Sloan-Kettering Cancer Center and himself an academy member and Nobel Prize winner. 'We may not be so good on the pipeline of producing new scientists, but the country is still a very effective magnet.'."[39] We note that in 2012 the Directors of both the NSF and DARPA were immigrants from India. In FY2012, they directed a combined total budget of US$8.6 billion for basic and applied research for the U.S. Government.[40]

University	Country 1	#	Country 2	#
MIT	India	6	United Kingdom	5
Stanford	Germany	3	India/China/France	2
UC Berkeley	India	4	Greece	3
Cal Tech	India	3	France/U.K.	2
U Michigan Ann Arbor	India	7	U.K.	6
Georgia Tech	India	10	China	6
U Illinois – Urbana Champaign	India	8	China	4
Purdue – West Lafayette	India	9	China	8
Cornell	China	4	Canada/Israel/U.K.	2
Princeton	U.K.	2	Australia/China/ Finland/Germany/ Italy/Lebanon/Poland	1
University of Maryland	India	7	China	4

(Source: Author's analysis of various online data from IEEE, ASME, Google, University websites and other relevant sources)

Table 3.11: Top 2 Countries of Origin for Foreign-born Faculty, # Foreign-born per Country per Institution

Country	Percentage
India	20%
China	13%
U.K.	10%
Greece	7%
France	5%

(Source: Author's analysis of various online data from IEEE, ASME, Google, University websites and other relevant sources)

Table 3.12: Top 5 Countries of Origin for Foreign-born Faculty across 11 Institutions

The benefit of immigration to the pool of well-educated S&E workers in the U.S. is clearly seen in publications such as NSF's *Why did they come to the United States? A Profile of Immigrant Scientists and Engineers*. A comparison between immigrant and native-born U.S. citizen counts from the report is shown in Table 3.14. The data show that immigrant scientists and engineers overall are educated at a higher level than those from the U.S.; are more likely to be educated in S&E fields (in particular in engineering, at nearly double the percentage of U.S. citizens); and, are more likely to then go on to work as scientists and engineers.

Born in U.S.	Born in U.S. (%)	Not born in U.S (%)
Estimates		
Total	84.5	15.5
Principal research field		
Agriculture and home economics	87.8	12.2
Business	75.2	24.8
Education	89.1	10.9
Engineering	**54.6**	**45.4**
Fine arts	90.5	9.5
Health sciences	79.4	20.6
Humanities	82.8	17.2
Natural sciences	67.2	32.8
Social sciences	82.9	17.1
All other programs	89.4	10.6
No scholarly activity	90.0	10.0

Table 3.13: Born in United States by Principal Research Field across (10) Categories[41]

Category	Native-born US Citizens (%)	Immigrants (%)
Highest Degree : Masters	27.1	30.2
Highest Degree : Doctorate	3.9	9.4
Highest Degree Field : S&E fields	53.5	62.5
Highest Degree Field : Engineering	11.5	21.6
Occupation : S&E occupations	20.1	30.5
Occupation : Engineers	6.8	9.4

Table 3.14: Immigrant S&E Profile[42]

Even in more general terms, high-skill immigrants have given much to the U.S. in terms of S&E fields – technology in particular, as explained in a 2009 study of immigrant impact on U.S. science and technology. Wadhwa et al. state that previous research showed that immigrants were CEOs or lead technologists in one of every four tech and engineering companies started in the United States from 1995 to 2005, and in 52 percent of Silicon Valley startups. These immigrant-founded companies employed 450,000 workers and generated $52 billion in revenue in 2006. The founders tended to be highly educated in STEM related disciplines, with 75 percent holding a Masters or Ph.D. degree.[43] The contribution of immigrants to industry in terms of founding companies in the U.S. is shown in Figure 3.2, showing a breakdown by industry – of note is the emphasis in engineering-based industries.

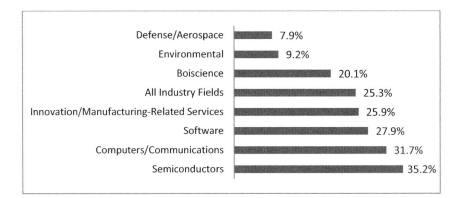

Figure 3.2: Percentage of Immigrant-Founded Companies by Industry, 2005[44]

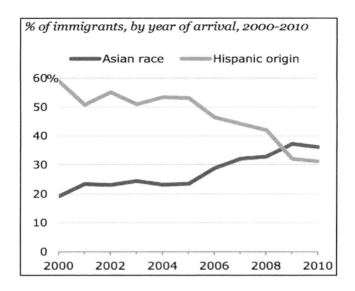

Figure 3.3: U.S. Immigration, Asian v. Hispanic, 2000-2010[45]

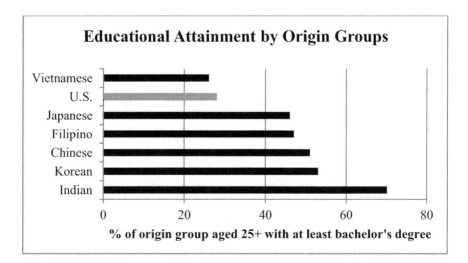

**Figure 3.4: Educational Attainment of Asian Immigrants in the U.S.
by Major Origin Group[46]**

In a June 2012 study of Asian American immigrants, often referred to as the 'model minority', researchers at the Pew Research Center found that Asian immigrants outnumbered Hispanic immigrants in 2010 as the most populous incoming group, as seen in Figure 3.3. This study also undertook an analysis of the educational attainment of recent Asian immigrants, as seen in Figure 3.4.

The study notes that 61% of Asian immigrant adults (25 to 64) in recent years have had at least a bachelor's degree. The authors note that, at double the share of non-Asian immigrants, this "almost surely makes the recent Asian arrivals the most highly educated cohort of immigrants in U.S. history."[47] The study found a number of additional positive characteristics of Asian immigrants.[48]

- They exceed all U.S. adults in college degrees (49% vs. 28%)
- They have a greater median annual household income ($66,000 vs. $49,800)
- They have greater median household wealth ($83,500 vs. $68,529)
- They have lower return migration rates than other immigrants
- They are more likely than other immigrants to be admitted on employment visas
- They received 45% of the engineering Ph.D. degrees granted in 2010, as well as 38% of Ph.D. degrees in math and computer sciences
- They hold 14% of S&E positions, yet they are only 5% of the U.S. population.

The U.S. appears to be well served in science and engineering by the Asian immigrant population, and it is believed that further immigration of this group would continue to bolster the field of engineering.

An Unexpected Value

Despite many studies performed by many different organizations on the value that immigrants add to the U.S. S&E workforce, the value added by their children to these fields is rarely analyzed. This is understandable, as information on the immigration status or history of parents is often not readily available.

Stuart Anderson discussed this topic in *The Multiplier Effect*, where he analyzed the immigration history of young competitors in three different top tier S&E competitions for high school students. He found that "foreign-born high school students make up 50 percent of the 2004 U.S. Math Olympiad's top scorers, 38 percent of the U.S. Physics Team, and 25 percent of the Intel Science Talent Search finalists – the United States' most prestigious awards for young scientists and mathematicians."[49]

Given the focus often trained on the required level of quality of the future S&E workforce for the U.S. rather than sheer numbers, it would appear that there are benefits to immigration reform in favor of greater numbers of S&Es in both the short term as well as the long term. Children of immigrants show a strong tendency to occupy the upper ranks of bright young students, as Anderson goes on to report that in 2004 "an astounding 60 percent of the top science students in the United States and 65 percent of the top math students are the children of immigrants."[50]

Using data from the U.S. Census Bureau's 2004 *Current Population Survey*,[51] we can see that if the talent and drive of foreign-born students were comparable to that of their U.S.-born peers, foreign students should represent only approximately 6.6% of the science and engineering fields. Instead, the data show for the U.S. Math Olympiad top scorers that immigrant students were greater than 7 times more likely than U.S.-born students to be in the upper echelon of high-skilled mathematics students. In addition, foreign-born students were almost 6 times more likely to be members of the U.S. Physics Team than their native-born peers; for the Intel Science Talent Search, they were almost 4 times more likely to be the highest achievers.

These are significant differences, and they reinforce the idea that foreign-born high school children in the U.S. are achieving at a higher performance level than native-born students in comparison to their total populations. This is not a new phenomenon; as part of a 1997 analysis of the lives of immigrant children, Min Zhou, a member of the Department of Sociology at the University of California, wrote that the list of top-ten award winners of the Westinghouse Science Talent Search had been dominated by second-generation immigrants over the previous 15 years.[52]

Stuart Anderson's follow-on brief in 2011, further studying children of immigrants and their representation in the U.S. Intel Science Talent Search competition, noted that based on interviews with finalists and parents, 70% of the 2011 Intel Science Talent Search finalists were children of immigrants. Anderson further found that "24 of the 28 immigrant parents started working in the United States on H-1B visas and later received an employer-sponsored green card. Fourteen of those 24 were international students."[53] His analysis of parental backgrounds revealed that out of the 40 children, 16 had immigrant parents from China and 10 from India, two countries previously noted to have heavy backlogs in visa applications. In our efforts to attract to best and brightest in science and engineering, there is clearly a future benefit and 'unexpected value' to the S&E field by increasing skilled immigration from these two countries.

Vivian Tseng, of the William T. Grant Foundation, writing in the *Journal of Child Development* in 2006, examined the correlation of immigrant status in children and their educational choices, and made a further point regarding the likelihood of immigrant children in the U.S. to choose an educational pathway in S&E fields. She stated that youths from immigrant families differed from their later-generation peers by pursuing college courses of study with higher math and science content. She further noted that growing evidence suggested that pursuing social and economic mobility through education was a prominent feature of the contemporary immigrant experience, and that studies had found that children of immigrants expressed higher educational motivation and aspirations than did their peers from U.S.-born families.[54]

Children of immigrants also have heavily engaged in entrepreneurship within the U.S. According to a May 2012 report from the Partnership for a New American Economy, a conservatively derived number is that "23 percent of the Fortune 500 firms, 114 companies, had at least one founder with an immigrant parent."[55] The study also noted that Fortune 500 companies founded by immigrants or children of immigrants employed more than 10 million people worldwide, and that the revenue directly generated by companies founded by children of immigrants in particular stood at US$2.5 trillion in 2010.[56]

However, some are also being lost back to more lucrative opportunities in growing economies abroad, as noted by Semple in April 2012. "In growing numbers, experts say, highly educated children of immigrants to the United States are uprooting themselves and moving to their ancestral countries. They are embracing homelands that their parents once spurned but that are now economic powers ... The United States government does not collect data specifically on the emigration of the American-born children of immigrants — or on those who were born abroad but moved to the United States as young children. But several migration experts said the phenomenon was significant and increasing."[57]

Conclusion

Historical science and engineering immigration data proved difficult to locate, primarily because many immigrants enter the U.S. through the "family" preference, rather than the more challenging "work-based" process.

Immigrants have filled positions and played a role in the U.S. at a level far above their representation in the population. There is no doubt we significantly benefit the U.S. in S&E by encouraging immigration to this country. It is overwhelmingly clear from the evidence that high-skill immigrants are an integral part of our highest S&E institutions, and indeed an integral part of the upper echelons of science and technology development in the U.S. – without their contributions, the U.S. would not be the technical leader it is today.

Both immigrants and their children 'hit above their weight' in the S&E field, as seen in an examination of major S&E competitions in the U.S. Both immigrants and their children were also found to be well represented in entrepreneurial ventures, founding companies in the U.S. that employ millions of people and generate trillions of dollars in revenue.

It was found that we may be losing many of the students who want to contribute much to S&E fields due to antiquated immigration laws that force them out, along with their U.S. educations. We are already seriously behind the level of immigration reform of many other countries, which are actively attempting to lure high skilled S&E students and workers in the new global marketplace to their countries – if we do not act we will lose our best and brightest to places where the available opportunities are more lucrative.

Relaxing immigration rules and increasing the number of allowed high-skill immigrant workers in science and engineering would result in an increase in the high-skilled S&E workforce for many years to come. The children of naturalized immigrants, whether brought here or born here, are more likely to both perform at a higher level than their U.S.-born peers in S&E pursuits, and choose S&E careers in higher numbers, particularly those in the Asian immigrant group.

As Vivek Wadhwa noted three years ago, "The United States is no longer the only place where talented people can put their skills to work. It can no longer expect highly skilled arrivals from other countries to endure the indignities and inefficiencies of an indifferent immigration system, and it must now actively compete to attract these people with good jobs, security, and other amenities."[58]

References

1. The Partnership for A New American Economy (2011). *The "New American" FORTUNE 500*. Retrieved from <http://www.renewoureconomy.org/sites/all/themes/pnae/img/new-american-fortune-500-june-2011.pdf>
2. Levin, D.B., Hill, K., and Warren, R. (1985). *Immigration Statistics: A Story of Neglect*, Panel of Immigration Statistics, Committee on

National Statistics, Commission on Behavioral and Social Sciences and Education, National Research Council.

3. Jefferys, K. (2004). *Characteristics of Employment-Based Legal Permanent Residents: 2004*. Retrieved from <http://www.dhs.gov/xlibrary/assets/statistics/publications/FSEmplo yBasedLPR2004.pdf>

4. National Science Foundation (2002). *Science and Engineering Indicators-2002.* Division of Science Resources Statistics, Arlington, VA: National Science Foundation (NSB-02-1).

5. Ibid.

6. Lazowska, E. (1995). *Is There a High-Tech Worker Shortage? A Review of the Evidence*. Retrieved from <http://www.cs.washington.edu/homes/lazowska/production.html>.

7. National Science Foundation (1996). *Immigrant Scientists, Engineers, and Technicians: 1993*. NSF 96-322 (Arlington, VA).

8. U.S. Department of Homeland Security, United States Citizenship and Immigration Services (2006). *Report on H-1B Petitions*. Retrieved from <http://www.uscis.gov/files/nativedocuments/H1B05Annual_08_7.p df>.

9. U.S. Citizenship and Immigration Services H1-B Cap press releases, various years, retrieved from <http://www.uscis.gov/>

10. U.S. Citizenship and Immigration Services (2010). "USCIS Cap count for H-1B, H-2B and H-3 Workers for Fiscal Year 2010", USCIS. Retrieved from <http://www.uscis.gov/h-1b_count>

11. U.S. Citizenship and Immigration Services (2012). "H-1B Specialty Occupations, DOD Cooperative Research and Development Project Workers, and Fashion Models". Retrieved from < http://www.uscis.gov/>

12. Stock, M.D. (2009). *Essential To The Fight : Immigrants In The Military Eight Years After 9/11*. Washington D.C. Immigration Policy Center. Retrieved from <http://immigrationpolicy.org/sites/default/files/docs/Immigrants_in _the_Military_-_Stock_110909_0.pdf>

13. Microsoft (2008). "Bill Gates Asks Congress to Act Now to Maintain U.S. Innovation Lead", retrieved from <http://www.microsoft.com/presspass/press/2008/mar08/03-12MSUSInnovationLeadPR.mspx>

14. Arrington, M. (2007). "TechCrunch interview with Barack Obama", TechCrunch, retrieved from <http://www.techcrunch.com/2007/11/26/qa-with-senator-barack-obama-on-key-technology-issues/>

15. "The 'SKIL' Bill : Short Title: Securing Knowledge Innovation and Leadership (SKIL)", retrieved from <http://cornyn.senate.gov/doc_archive/05-02-2006_SKIL%20section%20by%20section%20_5-1_.pdf>

16. Committee on Armed Services (2012). *National Defense Authorization Act for Fiscal Year 2013.* United States Senate, June 2012.

17. Wadhwa, V., Saxenian, A., Freeman, R., Gereffi, G., and Salkever, A. (2009) *America's Loss is the World's Gain: America's New Immigrant Entrepreneurs, Part IV* p. 6. Retrieved from <http://www.kauffman.org/uploadedfiles/americas_loss.pdf>

18. Orrenius, P. and Zavodny, M. (2010). From Brawn to Brains: How Immigration Works for America, *Federal Reserve Bank of Dallas, 2010 Annual Report*, retrieved from <http://www.dallasfed.org/assets/documents/fed/annual/2010/ar10b.pdf>.

19. Anderson, S. (2011). *Waiting and More Waiting: America's Family and Employment-Based Immigration System*, National Foundation for American Policy. Retrieved from <http://www.nfap.com/pdf/WAITING_NFAP_Policy_Brief_October_2011.pdf>

20. Pew Research Center (2012). The Rise of Asian Americans, *Social and Demographic Trends,* p. 27.

21. 112th Congress (2011-2012). "H.R. 3012: Fairness for High-Skilled Immigrants Act of 2011". Retrieved from <http://www.govtrack.us/congress/bills/112/hr3012>.

22. Harrison, J.D. (2012). Senators beckon immigrant entrepreneurs and workers with Startup Act 2.0. *Washington Post*, May 22, 2012. Retrieved from <http://www.washingtonpost.com/business/on-small-business/senators-beckon-immigrant-entrepreneurs-and-workers-with-startup-act-20/2012/05/22/gIQATplCjU_story.html>.

23. Moran, J. (2012). "Steve Case and Kauffman Foundation Join Senators to Introduce Startup Act 2.0", Press Releases, Jerry Moran, United States Senator for Kansas, retrieved from <http://moran.senate.gov/public/index.cfm/news-releases?ID=878f4a3a-1715-45f7-b01a-c98a11b9fd20>

24. Anderson, S. (2011). *Waiting and More Waiting: America's Family and Employment-Based Immigration System*, National Foundation for American Policy. Retrieved from <http://www.nfap.com/pdf/WAITING_NFAP_Policy_Brief_October_2011.pdf>

25. Institute of International Education (2011). *Open Doors 2011:Fast Facts*. Retrieved from <http://www.iie.org/en/Research-and-Publications/Open-Doors>

26. Villareal, A. (2010). Foreign Students Focus on Business, Engineering Studies in US Schools, *Voice of America*. Retrieved from <http://www.voanews.com/content/international-students-most-interested-in-us-business-engineering-programs---111391734/163039.html>.

27. Trotta, D. (2010). NY Mayor Bloomberg to promote immigration reform, *Reuters*. Retrieved from <http://www.reuters.com/article/2010/01/01/us-usa-immigration-bloomberg-idUSTRE6000ZJ20100101>.

28. Committee on Science, Security, and Prosperity, Committee on Scientific Communication and National Security Development, Security, and Cooperation, Policy and Global Affairs (2009). *Beyond 'Fortress America', National Security Controls on Science and Technology in a Globalized World*. National Research Council of the National Academies. Retrieved from <http://www.nap.edu/openbook.php?record_id=12567&page=R1>

29. Douglass, J.A., and Edelstein, R. (2009). *The global competition for talent - The rapidly changing market for international students and the need for a strategic approach in the U.S.*, Center for Studies in Higher Education, University of California, Berkeley. Retrieved from <http://cshe.berkeley.edu/publications/docs/ROPS.JD.RE.GlobalTalent.9.25.09.pdf>

30. National Science Foundation (2012). *Science and Engineering Indicators, 2012*. NSB 12-01 (Arlington, VA), Chapter 2, p. 2-5.

31. Kaspura, A. (2011). *The Engineering Profession, A Statistical Overview, Eighth Edition*, Engineers Australia. Retrieved from < http://www.engineersaustralia.org.au/sites/default/files/shado/Representation/Publications/Overview%20Document.pdf>

32. The Partnership for a New American Economy & The Partnership for New York City (2012). *Not Coming to America: Why the U.S. is falling behind in the global race for talent*. Retrieved from < http://www.renewoureconomy.org/sites/all/themes/pnae/not-coming-to-america.pdf>

33. Zakaria, F. (2012). Broken and Obsolete. *Time Magazine*, June 18. Retrieved from <http://class.povertylectures.com/BrokenObsoleteImmigrationPolicyFareedZakaria.pdf>

34. The Partnership for a New American Economy and The Partnership for New York City (2012). *Not Coming to America: Why the U.S. is*

falling behind in the global race for talent. Retrieved from < http://www.renewoureconomy.org/sites/all/themes/pnae/not-coming-to-america.pdf>

35. Ibid.
36. Ibid.
37. ASME (2012). "The 2010-2011 ASME Fellows". Retrieved from <http://files.asme.org/asmeorg/Governance/Honors/Fellows/31094.pdf>
38. US News and World Report (2010). *US News and World Report, Best Colleges 2010: Mechanical Engineering.* Retrieved from <http://colleges.usnews.rankingsandreviews.com/best-colleges/rankings/engineering-doctorate-mechanical>.
39. Fallows, J. (2010). How America can rise again. *The Atlantic*, January/February, p. 46.
40. FY2012 NSF budget retrieved from <http://www.aip.org/fyi/2011/137.html>, FY2012 Darpa budget retrieved from <http://www.darpa.mil/newsevents/budget.aspx>.
41. Heuer, R., et al. (2006). *2004 National Study of Postsecondary Faculty (NSOPF: 04) Methodology Report. Technical Report. NCES 2006-179.* National Center for Education Statistics.
42. Kannankutty, N. and Burrelli, J. (2007) *Why did they come to the United States? A Profile of Immigrant Scientists and Engineers.* NSF 07-324, June 2007, .p. 4.
43. Wadhwa, V., Saxenian, A., Freeman, R., Gereffi, G., and Salkever, A. (2009) *America's Loss is the World's Gain: America's New Immigrant Entrepreneurs, Part IV.* p.1. Retrieved from <http://www.kauffman.org/uploadedfiles/americas_loss.pdf>
44. Wadhwa, V. (2009). A Reverse Brain Drain, *Issues in Science and Technology*, Spring 2009, pp. 45-52.
45. Pew Research Center (2012). The Rise of Asian Americans, *Social and Demographic Trends*, June 19, p. 1.
46. Ibid.
47. Ibid.
48. Ibid.
49. Anderson, S. (2004). The Multiplier Effect. *International Education*, Summer, pp. 14-21. Retrieved from < http://www.nfap.net/researchactivities/studies/themultipliereffectnfap.pdf>
50. Ibid.
51. U.S. Census Bureau (2004). *2004 Current Population Survey.* Retrieved from <http://www.census.gov/cps/methodology/techdocs.html>

52. Zhou, M. (1997). Growing Up American: The Challenge Confronting Immigrant Children and Children of Immigrants, *Annu. Rev. Sociol.* 23, pp. 63–95.

53. Anderson, S. (2011). *The Impact of the Children of Immigrants on Scientific Achievement in America*, National Foundation for American Policy.

54. Tseng, V. (2006). Unpacking immigration in Youth's academic and occupational pathways. *Child Development*, 77(5), pages 1434–1445.

55. The Partnership for a New American Economy & The Partnership for New York City (2012). *Not Coming to America: Why the U.S. is falling behind in the global race for talent.* Retrieved from <http://www.renewoureconomy.org/sites/all/themes/pnae/not-coming-to-america.pdf>

56. The Partnership for A New American Economy (2011). *The 'New American' FORTUNE 500.* Retrieved from <http://www.renewoureconomy.org/sites/all/themes/pnae/img/new-american-fortune-500-june-2011.pdf>

57. Semple, K. (2012). Many U.S. Immigrants' Children Seek American Dream Abroad. *New York Times*, April 2012. Retrieved from <http://www.nytimes.com/2012/04/16/us/more-us-children-of-immigrants-are-leaving-us.html>.

58. Wadhwa, V. (2009). A Reverse Brain Drain. *Issues in Science and Technology*, Spring 2009, p. 51.

Chapter 4

Under-Represented Groups

"At present, you can't think of a black Bill Gates ... the Tiger Woods of computer science isn't out there."[1]

Increases in H-1B visa allocations, outsourcing, and off-shoring are either being considered or have been employed as pathways to providing a sufficient pool of talented S&Es to the United States. However, a significant portion of the U.S. population remains underrepresented in S&E employment, and more specifically in engineering. The following is an examination of the status of three sizable population groups that are underrepresented in engineering: women, African-Americans, and Latinos.[2] Women accounted for just 13 percent of all engineers across all engineering occupations in 2009, while African Americans were 5 percent and Latinos 6 percent;[3] yet, overall, members of these three groups account for 61 percent of the U.S. labor force aged 16 and older.

Several other population groups often included in examinations of engineering will not be featured in the present study. Although American Indians are also significantly underrepresented in engineering, the overall population is relatively small, so that the group impacts a handful of local labor markets rather than the national U.S. S&E workforce. While Asian-Americans also constitute a numerical minority within the U.S. population (4 percent), Asian Americans are not numerically underrepresented in engineering.[4] Finally, there has been much attention paid to increasing the participation of individuals with disabilities in STEM, in general. Disability status is an alterable individual characteristic, and the relative size of this population group varies with age – while about 12 percent of the U.S. population as a whole has a disability, 25 percent of those over age 65 have a disability.[5] Issues associated with access for individuals with disabilities are somewhat different than those that affect other groups underrepresented in STEM; therefore, we will not cover these issues in this volume.

John Brooks Slaughter, the first African-American director of the National Science Foundation, defines the 'New American Dilemma' as the relative absence of African Americans, Latinos and American Indians from scientific and engineering careers. He has noted that the obvious disparity in the representation of minorities and women is a growing problem for the STEM disciplines.[6] He further states:

> "... in the midst of the activity that has been spawned, in large part, by widely-read publications such as Thomas Friedman's book The World is Flat, and the national Academies' report, Rising Above the Gathering Storm, our leaders seem to have lost sight of the fact that there are many persons in America for whom participation in science and engineering has been, and in too many instances, continues to be less likely for a variety of reasons. And their numbers are growing dramatically ... In the numerous calls for immediate, strong and broad action to address the problems that have been identified, too little attention has been given to the recognition that steps to increase the presence of underrepresented minorities in the study of STEM courses could represent a part of the ultimate solution to the problem of the dwindling cohort of students entering the fields of science and engineering."[7]

As noted by the Department of Education in a report on the status and trends of education by race/ethnicity, the country's makeup is significantly different than it was 30 years ago. "Between 1980 and 2008, the racial/ethnic composition of the United States shifted – the White population declined from 80 percent of the total population to 66 percent; the Hispanic population increased from 6 percent of the total to 15 percent; the Black population remained at about 12 percent."[8] Figure 4.1 reflects projected population changes in the U.S. out to 2050.

The 'traditional' White male engineer template simply does not fit with the makeup of today's American population, and given the trend shown in Figure 4.1 and taking into consideration the growth in women's representation at all levels of education, the coming decades will find this template to be an even poorer fit. By relying solely on White males to populate engineering and other S&E fields, and failing to leverage the growing groups of both women and minorities completing undergraduate study, we are missing a significant opportunity to continue to grow the engineering workforce to maintain the preeminent position of the United States. As the NSF noted 2012, "postsecondary enrollment is projected to increase for all racial/ethnic groups, except for Whites. The proportion of White students is projected to decrease from 63% in 2008 to 58% by 2019, reflecting demographic changes."[9] For example, in 2010, 8.4% of bachelor's degrees conferred to White males were awarded in engineering, versus just 1.4% of females' bachelor's degrees. If women earned engineering degrees at the same rate as men – even if the total number of college degrees awarded remained unchanged but just the percentage awarded in engineering was on par with that of men – then our colleges and universities would generate an additional 65,812[10] engineering graduates. This is nearly twice the number of such degrees awarded to U.S. citizens and permanent residents, overall, in 2010.

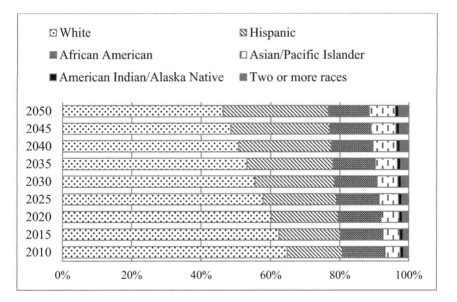

Figure 4.1: U.S. Population Composition by Race/Ethnicity, 2010 and Projected through 2050[11]

Women

According to 2010 U.S. Census data,[12] the 157 million women in the United States represent 51% of the population, and according to the Bureau of Labor Statistics, women accounted for just over 47% of the U.S. labor force aged 16 and older. According to the NSF, "Women have earned about 57% of all bachelor's degrees and half of all S&E bachelor's degrees since the late 1990s." Figure 4.2 illustrates this increase in young women's educational attainment. However, women are still underrepresented in computer sciences, mathematics, and engineering, while in other STEM fields, notably psychology, chemistry, and the life and social sciences, women earn more degrees than men.

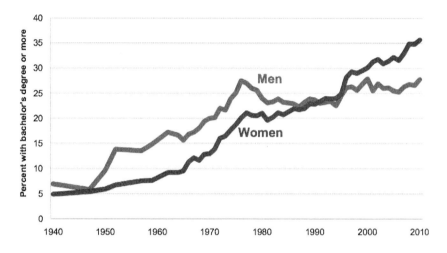

Figure 4.2: Percentage of 25-29 Year Old Men and Women with a Bachelor's Degree, 1940 to 2010[13]

Table 4.1 shows women's representation at various stages of postsecondary education. Data for representation in all fields and in the STEM fields, overall, provide a glimpse of the larger context into which women's participation in engineering fits. Women's undergraduate enrollment was relatively stable between 2001 and 2008, as shown in Table 4.1, hovering around 54%. In contrast, women's enrollment in engineering ranged from a high of 18% in 2001 to a low of 16% in 2004 and 2005.

Percent of Women at Various Postsecondary Education Levels, 2001-2010										
	2001	2002	2003	2004	2005	2006	2007	2008	2009	2010
First-time, full-time, - undergraduate enrollment in all fields (1)	53.5%	54.0%	54.2%	54.3%	54.6%	54.3%	54.2%	54.1%	N/A	N/A
Full-time undergraduate engineering enrollment (1)	18.3%	17.2%	16.4%	16.3%	16.2%	16.7%	16.8%	17.4%	N/A	N/A
Full-time graduate enrollment in all fields (2)	54.1%	54.6%	55.4%	56.4%	57.1%	57.5%	57.6%	57.3%	56.2%	N/A
Bachelor's all fields (2)	57.4%	57.6%	57.6%	57.6%	57.5%	57.6%	57.5%	57.4%	57.3%	57.2%
Bachelor's all STEM fields (2)	54.6%	54.7%	54.1%	54.3%	54.6%	55.1%	55.4%	55.7%	56.1%	56.2%
Bachelor's degrees, engineering (2)	20.1%	20.9%	20.3%	20.5%	20.0%	19.5%	18.5%	18.5%	18.1%	18.4%
Master's, all fields (2)	58.6%	58.8%	58.8%	59.0%	59.4%	60.1%	60.7%	60.6%	60.4%	60.3%
Master's, all STEM fields (2)	53.9%	54.0%	53.0%	52.9%	53.7%	55.0%	56.0%	56.3%	56.3%	56.9%
Master's degrees, engineering (2)	21.2%	21.2%	20.9%	21.1%	22.5%	23.2%	22.6%	23.0%	22.6%	22.3%
Doctoral, all fields (2)	45.0%	46.4%	47.2%	47.8%	48.8%	49.0%	50.2%	50.4%	50.6%	49.5%
Doctoral, all STEM fields (2)	40.0%	41.5%	42.5%	43.4%	45.0%	46.1%	47.1%	47.0%	47.1%	44.6%
Doctoral degrees, engineering (2)	16.6%	17.2%	17.2%	17.7%	18.7%	20.0%	20.9%	21.6%	21.6%	23.2%

Table 4.1: Women in Postsecondary Education

Sources: (1) National Science Foundation, Women, Minorities and persons with Disabilities in Science and Engineering (2012 update). (2) Author's Analysis of Integrated PostSecondary Education Data System (IPEDS) access value via the National Science Foundation WebCASPAR database system.

This enrollment level is consistent with 2010 data from the Higher Education Research Institute's (HERI) annual freshman survey. Figure 4.3 and Figure 4.4 show data from the most recent annual HERI survey. The first figure shows the sex ratios – computed by dividing men's percent by women's percent of students who reported intended majors – to illustrate the sex gaps in major choices. The sex gap in the report of intended major is largest for computer science; men are 7 times more likely than women to report this intended major. Engineering has the next largest gap, as 4.5 times as many men as women indicate that they plan to major in engineering. The other S&E fields are closer to parity, with women more likely than men to indicate that they plan to major in the biological/agricultural and social/behavioral sciences.

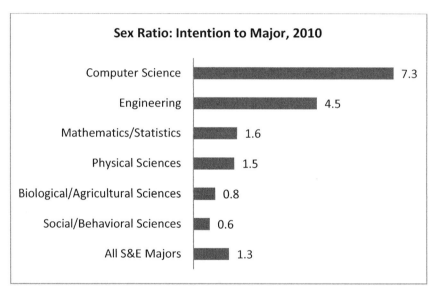

Sex ratio was computed as the percentage of men divided by the percentage of women who reported an intention to major in each field.
Source: Author's analysis of data from National Science Foundation (2012) Women, Minorities and Persons with Disabilities, updated tables, Table 2-8.

Figure 4.3: Sex Ratios: Intention to Major of New Undergraduates in Each S&E Field, 2010

The second chart shows the percentage of men and women, separated by race/ethnicity, who reported they intended to major in engineering or in the other STEM fields. Among the S&E fields, engineering is first-year men's top choice, with nearly 18% of first-time male undergraduates reporting that they intended to major in engineering. Just 4% of women reported that they intended to major in engineering, with differences among women of different racial/ethnic groups – 7% of Asian American women said they intended to major in engineering versus just 4% of White women, 3% of African American and Latino women, and under 2% of American Indian women.

So why are there so few women graduating in engineering? Longitudinal data from the 1980s demonstrated that women were far less likely than comparably-prepared men to major in engineering, but those who did, on average, had stronger academic records than their male counterparts.[14] In a more recent study, the Urban Institute compiled data on approximately 400,000 students in undergraduate engineering programs to investigate gender differences in retention. The study's authors noted that:

> *"...much to our surprise, we found that overall, and in most (but not all) engineering disciplines, women earn engineering degrees at rates equal to or higher than those of men. But the number of women enrolling in engineering is so small that even if all of them stuck with the major, we would still observe serious female under-representation. In a nutshell, the number of women studying engineering is simply too small."[15]*

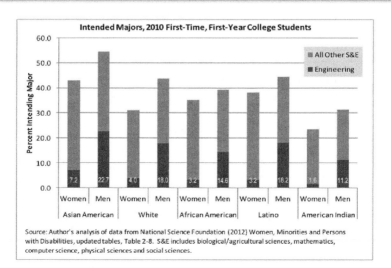

Source: Author's analysis of data from National Science Foundation (2012) Women, Minorities and Persons with Disabilities, updated tables, Table 2-8. S&E includes biological/agricultural sciences, mathematics, computer science, physical sciences and social sciences.

Figure 4.4: Intention to Major in S&E, 2010

For many years, engineering faculty and advocates for women in engineering fixated on differences in high school mathematics preparation, an argument that has been proven invalid for more than 20 years. As discussed in Chapter 2, relatively few Americans understand the work that engineers do, which has important implications for the gender gap. Without good information about the content of the work, inaccurate stereotypes or misinformation provide the basis upon which young people make decisions about engineering.[16] Values about occupations (that differ by gender and are formed prior to entering college, often quite early in life) appear to have an impact on whether women choose engineering.[17] Other researchers have emphasized various psychological factors such as confidence, resiliency, and stereotype threat.[18] Taken together, the literature suggests that increasing the public understanding of the reality of engineering may be a fruitful strategy to tapping a rich pool of female talent currently not being embraced by engineering colleges.[19]

It is important to note that at the doctoral level, more than half of engineering degrees – among women and men – are earned by non-U.S. citizens. While bachelor's and master's level engineers perform a number of important roles in the labor force, the work of engineers at the doctoral level is dramatically different from bachelor's and master's credentialed engineers. Engineering doctorates often perform work in research and development (R&D), typically qualitatively different work than that completed by engineers with other educational backgrounds. For the Department of Defense, this trend poses a special challenge in terms of identifying, nurturing and recruiting the R&D talent necessary to maintain the Nation's technological superiority for defense purposes. Figure 4.5 shows that the slow, steady upward trend in women's participation in doctoral-level engineering includes US women; and, recent increases in men's doctoral participation is due to U.S. and not foreign participation. Indeed, after September 11, 2001, foreign students encountered difficulties securing visas to study in the United States, hence the declines shown in Figure 4.5 for the number of doctoral degrees granted to foreign women and men in the period following 2007.[20]

Women's participation in the paid workforce, across all fields, grew from 30% in 1950 to 47% percent in 2010. According to the National Science Foundation, women represented 23% of the S&E workforce in 1993, growing to 27% in 2008,[21] an increase of just 4% over 15 years. There is, however, a danger in applying S&E statistics to engineering, as individual fields within the S&E grouping vary significantly. According to the NSF in 2012, "Female scientists and engineers are concentrated in different occupations than are men, with relatively high shares of women in the social sciences (53%) and biological and medical sciences (51%) and relatively low shares in engineering (13%) and computer and mathematical sciences (26%)."[22] In 2008, 204,000 females were employed in engineering occupations in the U.S., compared to 1,378,000 males – a significant gender imbalance at 13% female and 87% male.

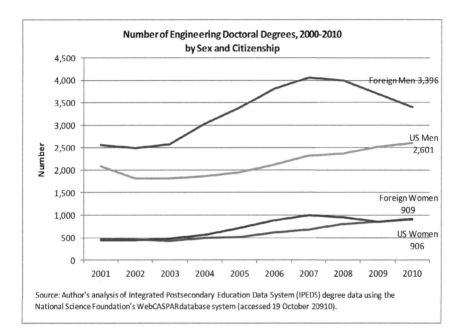

Figure 4.5: Number of Engineering Doctoral Degrees by Citizenship and Sex, 2000-2010

Retention in the engineering field after degree attainment is also a significant issue. Women are less likely than men to be retained in engineering employment, with some important differences observed across engineering fields, likely associated with structural forces in the larger economy.[23] Researchers have shown that negative working experiences impact women's retention in engineering.[24] Low female employment in science and engineering is not a uniquely U.S. problem; it is also an issue in other countries. For example, Pritchard states that in Australia, "the country faces a severe skills shortage, made even worse by an exodus of educated engineers to other occupations. Only 15% of qualified female engineers over 40 are still in the profession." Engineers Australia noted that recruitment of women is vital, as only 1 in 10 undergraduate engineering students in Australian universities are female.[25] Similar issues can be found in other developed countries, such as Canada, the U.K. and many Western European nations.[26]

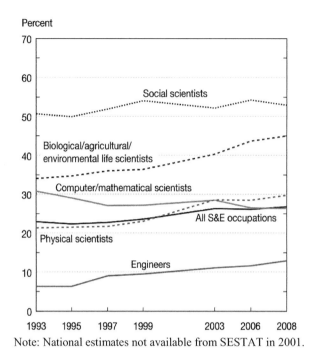

Note: National estimates not available from SESTAT in 2001.

Figure 4.6: Women in S&E Occupations, 1993 to 2008[27]

Retention in engineering was also the subject of a 2000 Congressional report on the advancement of women and minorities in S&E,[28] which found that women were twice as likely (25% vs. 12%) as their male colleagues to leave the engineering workforce after a few years. The women cited such reasons for leaving as these:

- Difficult balancing career and family
- Few female mentors
- Narrowly focused positions
- Inequality in management's evaluation of performance
- Exclusion from male-dominated upwardly mobile colleagues

A 2008 report by Hewlett et al. noted that 52% of highly credentialed women leave their positions in science, engineering and technology, and this attrition occurs primarily at mid-career (35-40 years old). The report

"If, and when, young women do get into the technology workforce, the pressures don't exactly let up. Although none of the female engineers I spoke with described explicitly hostile treatment while working in and around tech, many did acknowledge being acutely conscious of the low numbers of women — and, by extension, female mentors — around them. (Telle Whitney, president of the Anita Borg Institute, says that although about 21 percent of entry-level computer engineers are female, by the time you get to the top level, that number declines to 5.)"[29]

also found that the following five 'antigens' in corporate culture lead to this high rate of attrition:

- Hostile macho cultures
- Extreme work pressures
- Isolation
- Mysterious career paths
- Systems of risk and reward

To characterize factors related to respondents' career choices, Fouad and Singh surveyed 3,700 women between November 2009 and January 2011 who had graduated with engineering degrees. Workplace climate was cited as an important reason women either left engineering positions or avoided employment in engineering after graduation. The study noted that 15% of the participants in the survey chose not to work in the engineering field, citing perceptions of inflexibility in engineering and a workplace culture that was not supportive of women. Another 20% had started in careers in engineering but reported that they had been out of the field for at least five years at the time of their survey participation. The reasons for leaving engineering cited by Fouad and Singh's respondents were consistent with the 2000 congressional report and Hewlett et al. – working conditions, too much travel, lack of advancement or low salary were cited by nearly half of the respondents. A third of those who left engineering indicated that workplace climate, their boss, or the culture (in general) were reasons for leaving. Finally, 25% said they left to spend time with family.[30]

Other studies echo the findings from Fouad and Singh, documenting that in workplaces in which men are in the majority, such as those for female engineers (particularly in specialties such as mechanical engineering), women often face an uphill battle for acceptance and success. A 2010 report by the American Association of University Women[31] noted that traditional stereotypes that associate males with science and math and females with arts and humanities lead to implicit bias, even in the face of active rejection of such stereotypes. The report also found that people often have negative opinions of women in traditionally male positions unless they are clearly successful, at which point they are considered less likable, creating a double bind situation for females in S&E fields. Additionally, a 2008 *Harvard Business Review* article[32] found that 63% of science, engineering and technology workers reported suffering from sexual harassment in the workplace.

It is important to note, however, that attrition from engineering is not limited to women. Both men and women leave engineering for a number of career-related reasons. Engineering preparation provides individuals with strong analytical skills, which are useful in many types of positions outside engineering. Studies that rely on information provided only by women, then, are useful in showing what women think about the field, but they do not provide us with insight into a gender gap in perceptions about the field. That is, without knowing men's reasons for leaving the field, we have a limited view of how gender, specifically, impacts retention.

Recent work has shown that there are some differences in men's and women's retention in engineering. Men who leave engineering are more likely than women to cite pay and advancement opportunities as the principal reasons for leaving, while women are more likely to report that their career interests had changed.[33] As seen in Figure 4.7, for men in science, engineering and technology 'being highly compensated' was the primary driver; for women, the 'ability to contribute to society' was the primary motivator. These findings are consistent with the studies, cited earlier, about the reason women do not pursue engineering. That is, inaccurate understandings of engineering combined with the early development of sex differentiated occupational goals leave women's pathway into engineering unpaved.

Underrepresented Ethnic Minority Groups

Three large population categories are included in most analyses of underrepresented minority groups in STEM: African Americans, American Indians and Alaska Natives, and Latinos.[34] As shown in Table 4.2, women represented 47% of the U.S. labor force in 2010 and were, in general, overrepresented in the professional and related occupations (57.5%). However, when drilling down within the professional occupations to engineering, specifically, the representation of women was much smaller. The representation of Blacks among professional workers is almost at parity to workforce representation, but participation in engineering is much smaller. Latinos are the least likely category shown in the table to be employed in professional occupations. Latino representation among engineers is slightly higher than that of Blacks, but it is still far below the parity level compared to the relative size of the U.S. Latino labor force (14%). Asians, for comparison purposes, are overrepresented among professional occupations and in each of the four engineering categories.

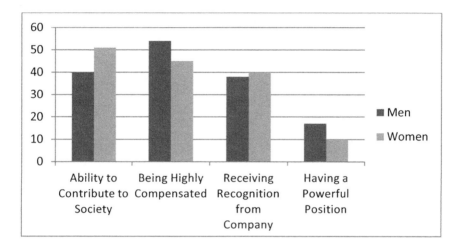

Figure 4.7: Prime Motivators for SET Talent[35]

	Number	Percent Female	Percent Black	Percent Hispanic	Percent Asian
Total U.S. labor force(1)	139,877,000	47.3%	10.7%	14.0%	4.7%
Professional and related(1)	30,690,000	57.5%	9.4%	7.1%	7.1%
Engineering managers(2)	144,210	8.7%	2.5%	3.3%	9.5%
Engineers(2)	1,698,802	12.3%	4.5%	5.5%	12.7%

Engineering technicians(2)	681,036	17.5%	7.0%	8.7%	6.3%
Sales engineers(2)	28,848	4.0%	1.6%	5.2%	7.8%
All engineering occupations(2)	2,552,896	13.4%	5.0%	6.2%	10.7%

Note: Female includes females of all race/ethnic categories. Likewise, the race/ethnic category data include females and males within those categories.
Sources: (1) U.S. Census Bureau Statistical Abstract of the United States, 2010.
(2) Author's Analysis of 2009 American Community Survey PUMS data.

Table 4.2: Number of Engineers and Representation of Women and Minorities, 2010[37]

As shown in Figure 4.8 and Figure 4.9, the number of underrepresented minorities receiving engineering bachelor's degrees has slowly but steadily increased among Latinos and American Indians/Alaska Natives. Among African Americans, however, the growth of the number of engineering bachelor's degrees ceased in the late 1990s: since then the number of African Americans earning bachelor's degrees has remained relatively stable through 2010 (the latest available data).

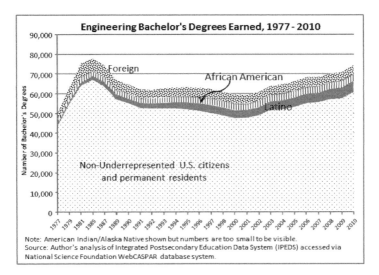

Figure 4.8: Number of Engineering Bachelor's Degrees by Population Category, 1977-2010

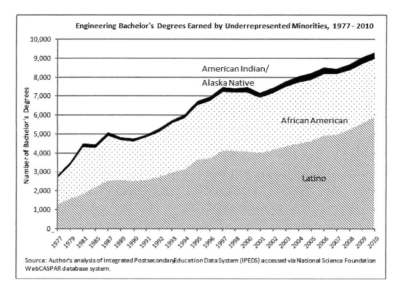

Figure 4.9: Number of Engineering Bachelor's Degrees Earned by Underrepresented Minorities, 1977-2010

Because sex differences in high school preparation have fundamentally disappeared, the belief that women do not pursue engineering due to low mathematics achievement is simply not valid. In contrast, the low level of mathematics preparation is, indeed, a key factor in Latinos' and African Americans' persistently low level of participation in engineering. Another point of departure when comparing women's participation in engineering to that of African Americans or Latinos is that, whereas women are, indeed, overrepresented in some of the other STEM fields (e.g., biological/agricultural sciences) and the representation of women varies greatly across the STEM fields, members of the three underrepresented minority (URM) groups are underrepresented in all STEM fields, far below labor force or age group parity. Despite accounting for 34% of 18-24 year olds, members of the three chief underrepresented groups – African Americans, American Indians/Alaska Natives, and Latinos – accounted for just 13% of U.S. citizens and permanent residents who earned bachelor's degrees in engineering in 2010.[37]

As shown in Figure 4.10, U.S. high school students from all racial/ethnic groups are increasingly likely to complete a rigorous high school curriculum, but there are large differences across racial/ethnic groups. A rigorous curriculum has been shown to be a key factor in student success in college and consists of four years of English, three years of social studies, four years of mathematics (including pre-calculus or higher), three years of science (including biology, chemistry, and physics), and three years of foreign language. Only a small percentage of African American and Latino students complete such a curriculum – 6% and 8%, respectively, in 2009. It should also be noted, however, that only 14% of White students complete this foundational set of classes. Between 2005 and 2009, though, as the percentage of Asian American and White students completing a rigorous high school curriculum increased, there was no such increase among African American and Latino students.

Without the preparation of a rigorous high school curriculum, African American and Latino students who go to college are more likely to struggle with their classes. As shown in Figure 4.11, retention to graduation among students who enter college to major in engineering, engineering technology or computer science[38] as of 2009 was lowest for African Americans in the 2003-04 entering class. Data in Figure 4.11 are from the Beginning Postsecondary Student Survey, a nationally-representative longitudinal survey of college students. Just over half of Latino students persisted to earn a bachelor's degree in engineering, engineering technology, or computer science by 2009; but only 31% of African American students were successful in completing a bachelor's degree in these fields. Indeed, African American students were as likely to leave college without earning any credential as they were to complete a bachelor's degree, with another 22% continuing to work towards a degree in 2009.

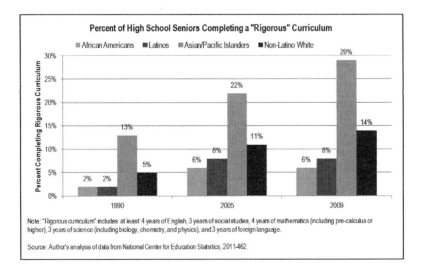

Figure 4.10: Trends in Completion of a Rigorous High School Curriculum

> *"Most of the city's (Alexandria, VA) students are black or Hispanic. Most in gifted programs are white. This imbalance in classes tailored to gifted and talented students is echoed across the region and the nation, a source of embarrassment to many educators."[39]*

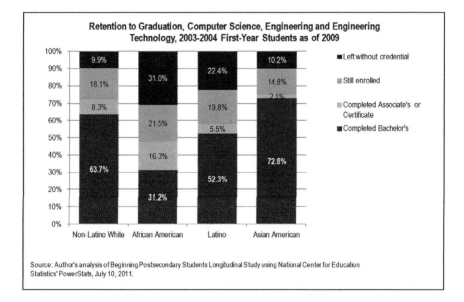

Figure 4.11: Completion of 2003-04 College Freshmen as of 2009 by Race/Ethnicity

Research by Bowen, Chingos and McPherson indicates that even though educational aspirations are similar across racial/ethnic and socioeconomic status (SES) groups, there is still a wide gap in college completion. In particular, among students from the top income quintile with at least one parent who completed college, 68% complete college by the time they are 26 years old. But, for those from the lowest income quintile who do not have a parent who completed college, only 9% completed a bachelor's degree by their 26th birthday. Bowen et al. show that high school grades are predictive of college success, as they reflect the study and time-management skills – beyond subject matter content – that are critical to success in college.[40] Bowen and his colleagues confirm others' findings that the 3.0 grade point average is a cut-off point; students who earn at least a 3.0 are far more likely to graduate from college than those who fall just below that point.

> *"Latino youths are one of the country's fastest-growing demographic groups: In the past 20 years, the number of Latinos younger than 18 has doubled to 16 million. One-fifth of children in the United States today are Latino, and 92 percent of them are US citizens. By 2035, one-third of all children in the country will be Latino."*[41]

Latino/Hispanic

People who classified themselves as 'Latino' or 'Hispanic' comprised 16% of the U.S. population in 2010, making them the largest racial/ethnic minority category. The Latino/Hispanic population grew by 43% between 2000 and 2010, approximately four times the growth of the overall U.S. population over the same period. Accounting for 60% of the growth in numbers of public school students from 2000-2010, Latinos/Hispanics are projected to replace Whites as the majority of California's population by the year 2042, and to represent 30% of the total U.S. population in 2050. An editorial in the ASEE magazine, *Prism*, suggests that the implications of Latino/Hispanic population growth are important for engineering schools, as "with the chasm threatening to grow even wider in just a few short years, many engineering educators say that attracting more Hispanics to engineering education is no longer a matter of choice."[42]

Latino/Hispanic undergraduate enrollment has grown steadily from 2001 to 2010, as shown in Table 4.3. Representation of Latino/Hispanic students in the overall first-time, full-time undergraduate population rose from 10% in 2001 to 14% in 2010, as shown in Table 4.3. Graduate enrollment of Latinos/Hispanics, both in general and in engineering, has shown little progress over the past decade. Indeed, all of the trends in

Table 4.3 show little progress in the representation of Latinos at all degree levels, both overall and in engineering in particular.

According to research by ¡Excelencia! in Education,[43] Hispanic students face significant hurdles in completing bachelor's degree programs in engineering, including language barriers, immigration issues, family expectations, aversion to debt, and other issues often common to first-generation college students. Hispanic Serving Institutions (HSIs) have attempted to address some of these issues to increase Hispanic enrollment and graduation rates. As with other minorities, a lack of role models and mentors is problematic for Hispanic students, and while a large number of Hispanic engineers occupy high profile positions, their visibility is still low, an issue that the Society of Hispanic Professional Engineers (SHPE) is working to correct.

While HSIs are important in the production of Latino/Hispanic college graduates, the extent to which they truly serve Latino/Hispanic students varies greatly. But according to a report by Excelencia in Education: "Latino college students' choices create HSIs. However most Latino students enrolled at HSIs did not know their institution was an HSI."[44] This means the institutions that "count" as HSIs can change each year, depending on the percentage of Latino students among enrolled students. In fact, by emphasizing college costs, proximity, and accessibility when selecting a college or university, Latino/Hispanic students have been responsible for creating the 236 HSIs in the United States, which, by definition, enroll at least 25% undergraduate Latino/Hispanic full-time students.

According to Excelencia, Latino students who attended HSIs were attracted by their open admissions policies and accessible locations in communities with large Latino populations. Latino students who did not attend HSIs were more likely to be motivated by financial aid, institutional prestige and academic programs in making their enrollment decisions. In order for colleges and universities to better serve the growing Latino/Hispanic student population, they should take steps to satisfy the criteria those students value most when choosing a college (i.e., cost, proximity and an accessible campus).

To capture Latino student perspectives on college and college choices, Excelencia conducted focus groups and interviews with 103 Latino students across the country. These discussions suggest some immediate steps colleges and universities can take to improve the recruitment of Latino students, including:

- Enlisting the support of current Latino college students by making them available to high school students as information resources

Percent of Latinos/Hispanics at Various Postsecondary Education Levels, 2001-2010										
	2001	2002	2003	2004	2005	2006	2007	2008	2009	2010
First-time, full-time, undergraduate enrollment in all fields (1)	10.4%	10.7%	11.0%	11.4%	11.7%	12.2%	12.4%	13.6%	N/A	N/A
Full-time graduate enrollment in all fields (2)	4.0%	4.1%	4.4%	4.5%	4.6%	4.6%	4.6%	4.5%	4.6%	4.8%
Full-time graduate enrollment in engineering (2)	2.3%	2.3%	2.5%	2.8%	2.8%	2.9%	2.8%	2.5%	2.7%	3.0%
Bachelor's all fields (2)	7.2%	7.3%	7.4%	7.5%	7.7%	7.9%	8.1%	8.3%	8.5%	8.8%
Bachelor's all STEM fields (2)	6.9%	7.1%	7.3%	7.3%	7.4%	7.5%	7.7%	8.0%	8.2%	8.5%
Bachelor's degrees, engineering (2)	6.8%	6.8%	6.8%	6.9%	7.0%	7.2%	7.3%	7.5%	7.9%	8.0%
Master's, all fields (2)	4.8%	4.8%	4.9%	5.3%	5.6%	5.7%	6.0%	5.9%	6.1%	6.2%
Master's, all STEM fields (2)	4.1%	4.2%	4.2%	4.5%	4.7%	4.9%	5.1%	5.0%	5.0%	5.3%
Master's degrees, engineering (2)	3.2%	3.3%	2.9%	3.3%	3.4%	3.4%	3.9%	3.7%	3.6%	3.8%
Doctoral, all fields (2)	3.5%	3.4%	3.5%	3.6%	3.6%	3.5%	3.5%	3.9%	3.9%	4.0%
Doctoral, all STEM fields (2)	3.2%	3.0%	3.1%	3.4%	3.3%	3.2%	3.2%	3.6%	3.2%	3.6%
Doctoral degrees, engineering (2)	1.6%	1.7%	2.0%	1.7%	1.5%	1.4%	1.7%	1.6%	1.9%	2.5%

Sources: (1) National Science Foundation, Women, Minorities and persons with Disabilities in Science and Engineering (2012 update). (2) Author's Analysis of Integrated PostSecondary Education Data System (IPEDS) access value via the National Science Foundation WebCASPAR database system.

Table 4.3: Latino/Hispanic Representation at Various Stages of Postsecondary Education, All Fields, STEM, and Engineering, 2001-2010

- Engaging entire families in the process by developing and disseminating information to students and parents that explains what students will be doing in college
- Providing reliable and quality information by increasing the numbers of quality high school guidance counselors so that more than the "top 5%" of students get solid college guidance.

African Americans

African-Americans comprised 13% of the U.S. population in 2010 according to U.S. Census data. Loftus states that "while the stream of African-Americans going into engineering has slowly increased since the 1970s, the numbers have leveled off in recent years, even as the number of Latinos/Hispanics has edged up slightly. One fourth of African-Americans still live in poverty. Set against the country's overall engineering shortage, which will be exacerbated in coming years by the retirement of baby boomers, the need to tap into the potential of underrepresented minorities has become more urgent-both for educators and industry."[45]

For African Americans, the first decade of the 21st century indicates little change in the relative share in enrollment – at both the undergraduate and graduate levels – or in the share of degrees in all fields, in the STEM fields and in engineering. There has been a slight increase in African American participation in graduate education overall but not in the STEM fields or engineering, which show slight decreases over the 10-year period.

Historically Black Colleges and Universities (HBCUs) have always been critical institutions for African Americans, including in engineering fields. As shown in Table 4.5, according to a National Action Council for Minorities in Engineering (NACME) analysis of IPEDS degree data for 2009, five of the top ten producers of African American engineers at the bachelor's level were HBCUs: North Carolina A&T, Morgan State University, Prairie View A&M, Southern University A&M, and Tuskegee University. It should be noted, too, that African American women's representation among bachelor's degree graduates at these institutions is much higher than the overall percentage of women among engineering bachelor's degrees (18%). At North Carolina A&T, for example, African American women earned 37% of the engineering bachelor's degrees awarded to African Americans at this HBCU in 2009, and at Georgia Tech in that same year, African American women earned 31% of engineering bachelor's awarded to African Americans. African American women's participation in engineering has been relatively strong since the late 1980s.

Percent of African Americans at Various Postsecondary Education Levels, 2001-2010	2001	2002	2003	2004	2005	2006	2007	2008	2009	2010
First-time, full-time, undergraduate enrollment in all fields (1)	11.3%	11.5%	11.8%	12.0%	12.1%	12.0%	12.2%	12.6%	N/A	N/A
Full-time graduate enrollment in all fields (2)	4.3%	4.3%	4.4%	4.6%	4.6%	4.8%	4.6%	4.9%	4.9%	4.9%
Full-time graduate enrollment in engineering (2)	2.1%	2.1%	2.0%	2.3%	2.3%	2.4%	2.3%	2.2%	2.2%	2.2%
Bachelor's all fields (2)	8.5%	8.5%	8.6%	8.7%	8.8%	8.9%	8.9%	9.0%	9.0%	9.1%
Bachelor's all STEM fields (2)	8.6%	8.7%	8.7%	8.8%	8.8%	8.7%	8.9%	8.7%	8.7%	8.7%
Bachelor's degrees, engineering (2)	4.9%	4.9%	4.8%	5.0%	4.8%	4.7%	4.6%	4.4%	4.4%	4.1%
Master's, all fields (2)	7.5%	7.6%	7.8%	8.0%	8.5%	8.8%	9.1%	9.1%	9.3%	9.6%
Master's, all STEM fields (2)	6.4%	6.5%	6.7%	6.8%	7.0%	7.3%	7.7%	7.8%	7.8%	8.3%
Master's degrees, engineering (2)	2.6%	2.8%	2.8%	2.5%	2.6%	2.7%	3.0%	2.9%	2.7%	2.9%
Doctoral, all fields (2)	4.6%	5.1%	5.1%	5.6%	5.4%	5.1%	5.7%	5.6%	5.9%	5.9%
Doctoral, all STEM fields (2)	3.0%	3.2%	3.1%	3.4%	3.1%	3.2%	3.2%	3.3%	3.6%	3.4%
Doctoral degrees, engineering (2)	1.8%	1.5%	1.8%	1.7%	1.5%	1.5%	1.5%	1.6%	1.8%	2.0%

Sources: (1) National Science Foundation, Women, Minorities and Persons with Disabilities in Science and Engineering (2012 update). (2) Author's analysis of Integrated PostSecondary Education Data System (IPEDS) access value via the National Science Foundation WebCASPAR database system.

Table 4.4: African American Representation at Various Stages of Postsecondary Education: All Fields, STEM, and Engineering, 2001-2010

Rank	Institution	Carnegie Classification of Institution	Women	Men	Total
1	North Carolina Agricultural & Tech State Univ*	Research Universities (high research activity)	53	92	145
2	Georgia Institute of Technology, Main Campus	Research Universities (very high research activity)	34	77	111
3	Morgan State University (Maryland)*	Doctoral/Research Universities	21	50	71
4	Prairie View A&M University (Texas)*	Master's Colleges and Universities	24	42	66
5	North Carolina State University at Raleigh	Research Universities (very high research activity)	22	40	62
6	Southern University A&M Col at Baton Rouge*	Master's Colleges and Universities	17	41	58
7	University of Maryland at College Park	Research Universities (very high research activity)	6	47	53
8	University of Michigan at Ann Arbor	Research Universities (very high research activity)	24	26	50
9	Tuskegee University (Alabama)*	Baccalaureate Colleges	9	39	48
10	University of Florida	Research Universities (very high research activity)	22	26	48
11	Alabama Agricultural and Mechanical University*	Master's Colleges and Universities	8	39	47
12	Florida Agricultural and Mechanical University*	Doctoral/Research Universities	10	32	42
13	Virginia Polytechnic Institute and State Univ	Research Universities (very high research activity)	9	30	39
14	University of Missouri, Rolla	Research Universities (high research activity)	12	27	39
15	CUNY City College	Master's Colleges and Universities	10	27	37
16	Florida Atlantic University	Research Universities (high research activity)	2	28	30
17	Louisiana State Univ & Agric & Mechanical Col	Research Universities (very high research activity)	9	21	30
18	George Mason University (Virginia)	Research Universities (high research activity)	3	26	29
19	University of Central Florida	Research Universities (high research activity)	3	25	28
20	University of South Florida	Research Universities (very high research activity)	4	24	28

*indicates Historically Black College or University (HBCU); #1,2 are institutions at which African Americans earned 100 or more bachelor's degrees in engineering;
#3 to 8 are those where African Americans earned 50-99 bachelor's degrees in engineering.
Sources: NACME analysis of IPEDS data accessed via NSF WebCASPAR database system, June 2011.

Table 4.5: Top Institutions Conferring Engineering Bachelor's Degrees to African Americans, 2009[46]

Even though HBCUs have helped enroll and retain more Black students, issues with poverty, racial/social isolation, and a lack of preparation for college significantly impact African-American student enrollment and persistence in S&E fields in general, and in engineering in particular. African American students especially struggle at predominantly White institutions where they and their families continue to encounter racist attitudes and a lack of support.[47]

African Americans and Latinos in the Engineering Workforce

Table 4.6 summarizes relative participation in S&E occupations by race/ethnicity, for 1993 to 2008. Hispanic representation in S&E has increased from 2.9% in 1993 to 4.9% in 2008. African American participation in S&E increased only modestly, while that of American Indians/Alaska Natives was relatively stable. By 2008, Whites represented slightly less than 72% of S&Es in the U.S. workforce, a decline from 84% in 1993. A concurrent increase in the representation of Asian and Pacific Islanders (almost entirely due to the participation of Asians rather than Pacific Islanders) over the same 15-year period is the principal reason for the declining representation of Whites among U.S. S&E workers.

Race	1993	1995	1997	1999	2003	2006	2008
Hispanic	2.9%	2.8%	3.1%	3.4%	4.4%	4.6%	4.9%
Black	3.6%	3.4%	3.4%	3.4%	4.3%	3.9%	3.9%
American Indian/Alaska Native	0.2%	0.3%	0.3%	0.3%	0.3%	0.4%	0.3%
Asian/Pacific Islander	9.1%	9.6%	10.4%	11.0%	14.5%	16.6%	17.3%
White	84.1%	83.9%	82.9%	81.8%	75.2%	73.2%	71.8%

Table 4.6: Distribution of Workers in S&E Occupations, by Race and Year, 1993 to 2008[48]

Workforce discrimination is still an issue for women and members of racial/ethnic minority groups and can be especially problematic for women of color. For example, Hispanic women S&Es, in particular, face discrimination, lower salaries, and in some cases hostile work environments. According to NSF data, Hispanic women are paid 10 to 13 percent less, on average, than other female engineers. Language barriers are also cited as an issue: "Some Hispanic women are not taken seriously by peers or supervisors. Many times it is due to their accent, which may lead to communication problems," states Christella Chavez, a manufacturing engineer with Visteon Corp. in Tulsa, Oklahoma.[49] For either gender, even the stigma of being Hispanic, a racial connection with illegal and legal immigrants who often do low level manual labor work in American society, can be a detrimental factor for both males and females in S&E fields. As noted by Ivan Favila, a Hispanic mechanical engineer and Assistant Dean of the College of Engineering at University of Illinois at Urbana-Champaign, "It would be naïve to say that once someone receives their [sic] engineering degree, their personal and professional problems are solved. There are issues that all graduates have to deal with: corporate politics, access to positions of power, appropriate mentorship, and avenues for growth and recognition. It is also naïve to say that these issues are unaffected by social and racial preferences."[50]

Black students and workers in S&E fields also face specific cultural issues. African-American workers still face issues of racism in subtle and unspoken forms in the workplace, an unfortunate lingering reality of some traditionally White-dominated S&E workplaces.[51]

Beyond the group-specific strategies suggested earlier, there are many efforts that seek to close the gap in Latino and African American participation in engineering. Such organizations as those described in the box (i.e., SWE, NSBE, SHPE and NACME) feature programs that reach out to young people to provide them and their families with more information about engineering to encourage them to get on and stay on a pathway through a rigorous high school curriculum so that they can more efficaciously pursue engineering in college.

The National Math and Science Initiative (NMSI), among others programs, is working to rectify the disparity in students' college preparation often associated with the continued tracking of minority and low-income students into lower-level high school courses.[52] NMSI grant funds provide support for students to have preparation sessions and extra coursework at local universities. An article in *Prism* highlighted one example where a student at Malden High School in Massachusetts was able to take extra preparatory courses at Northeastern University in order to be prepared for college engineering.

Minority enrollment in AP classes has surged in the six states where the National Math and Science Initiative's AP Training and Incentive Program (APTIP) is underway. Again, according to Loftus, writing in 2009, "While AP enrollment in NMSI-participating high schools has climbed by 70% overall, for African-American and Hispanic students, it has leapt a stunning 122%. In Dallas, where NMSI is based and where the idea behind APTIP first took off, the overall number of students who received passing scores on math, science, and English AP exams in 10 participating high schools reached 1,466 in 2007 – nine times the level of 1995. The number of under-represented minority students who passed the exam was 20 times that of 1995."[53] Further, 2008-2011 results from 63 schools in six states showed a 124 percent average increase in passing rates on math, science and English AP exams at 63 schools – nearly six times the national average. A 216 percent increase in passing scores on math, science and English AP exams among African-American and Hispanic students was achieved, over four times the national average, and the passing rate for female students increased 144 percent – over seven times the national average.[54]

These encouraging results have helped boost hope that NMSI, a public-private partnership funded primarily by Exxon-Mobil, may succeed where previous STEM efforts have not. In late 2011 the group merged with the Laying the Foundation (LTF) teacher training organization, and now appears ready to support students from high school to college in a comprehensive approach to improving STEM performance.

The National Action Council for Minorities in Engineering (NACME) partnered with the National Academies Foundation and Project Lead the Way (PLTW) to develop "engineering academies" at high schools with high African American, Latino or American Indian/Alaska Native enrollment. These academies provide access to corporate role models from NACME's partner companies so that young people can learn, firsthand, about the work that engineers do. In addition, the academies implement the PLTW high school engineering curriculum, which gives students a hands-on taste of engineering.

A Case Study: University of Maryland

We reviewed the trends for the period of 2000 to 2007 of various groups of students entering universities to specifically study engineering. To do this, we gathered data on undergraduate students at the national, university, college, and department levels, using the University of Maryland, College Park, as a "sample" university due to its 18th position ranking by *U.S. News and World Report* in 2012 amongst engineering programs in the country, and relative ease of access to information. The total number of students and their race/ethnicity and gender were the categories identified as important for analysis, and the period of 2000 to

2010 was selected as the date range for historical data to best illustrate past trends.

Figures 4.12 through 4.15 show the trends of students enrolled in both engineering and all subjects. Figure 4.12 shows that although half of college freshman at both the University of Maryland and at a national level were female, only 10-20% were engineering freshmen. Figure 4.13 shows that approximately 70% of engineering freshmen were White, which is consistent with the national data. Figure 4.14 shows that African American students' representation was declining in engineering. The College of Engineering at the University of Maryland is particularly interesting, because from 1993 to 1999 an African-American Associate Dean of Student Affairs, Brigadier General Horace L. Russell, took considerable interest in mentoring Black students in the department, and developed a successful minority program that had a significant effect on African American student enrollment. Once he retired, however, African American student enrollment dropped back to national levels, with a subsequent decline in representation. Consistent with the national trend, the representation of Hispanic students increased slightly, as shown in Figure 4.15. Hispanics were not as well-represented among engineering students at the University of Maryland as they were nationwide.

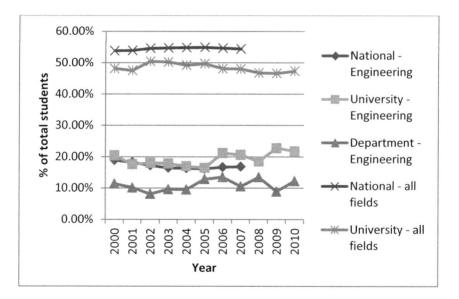

Figure 4.12: Gender: Female, Full-time First-year Undergraduates in Engineering vs. all Fields (% of Total)[55]

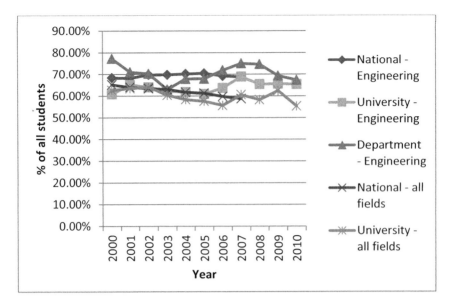

Figure 4.13: Race: White, Full-time First-year Undergraduates in Engineering vs. all Fields (% of Total)

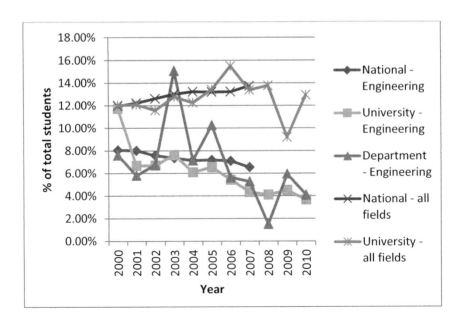

Figure 4.14: Black/African American, Full-time First-year Undergraduates in Engineering vs. all Fields (% of Total)

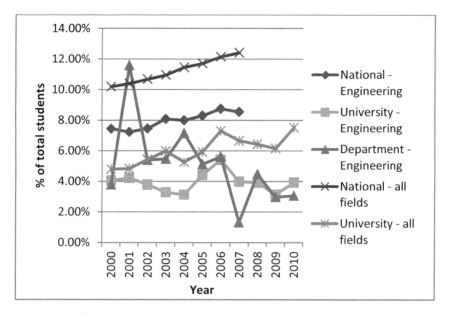

Figure 4.15: Hispanic, Full-time First-year Undergraduates in Engineering vs. all Fields (% of Total)

Community colleges can play a very significant role in preparing all students, especially minority students, to successfully complete engineering baccalaureate degrees. Dowd et al. state that community colleges have:

> "Latino community college transfers who first earn associate's degrees have lower access to STEM bachelor's degrees at academically selective and private universities than their counterparts who do not earn an associate's degree prior to the bachelor's degree. Transfer students were more likely to graduate from HSIs (32.1% with an associate's degree compared to 16.8% without one) and from public four-year institutions (83% as opposed to 62.9%). However, they were less likely to graduate from academically selective institutions (42% with an associate's degree compared to 59% without one) or from research universities (25.3% as opposed to 43.5%)."[56]

According to the National Academies report *Enhancing the Community College Pathway to Engineering Careers*, articulation agreements, careful attention to curricular content and quality, and attention to the issues for the more "non-traditional" community college students are important steps to forge a stronger connection between the community colleges and engineering schools.[57] A NACME-sponsored study found that community college transfer students in engineering actually performed better than their peers who had gone straight to a four-year school after high school. Faculty at the four-year colleges who took students as transfer students appreciated the maturity and tenacity of the transfer students as well as their strong technical skills.[59]

NACME's John Brooks Slaughter cites a number of key points in favor of minority participation at community colleges, including affordability, proximity to communities, a greater balance in faculty demographics, smaller class sizes and greater levels of faculty interaction, a more collaborative environment, and flexibility. He also makes the point that there must be greater emphasis on the ability to transfer community college degrees to 4 year institutions. Dowd et al. again note, however, that:

> "… largely been overlooked in the national dialogue on how to increase the number of Latinas and Latinos in STEM careers. Latinos are more likely to attend community college than are members of other racial ethnic groups and nearly 60% of all Latinos enrolled in postsecondary education attend a community college. Latino college students also tend to be concentrated in a small number of institutions, which are predominantly HSIs. Only 10% of the four-year institutions of higher education in the United States enroll the majority (54%) of Latino undergraduates. Any effort to increase the number of Latino STEM degree holders will depend on the institutional capacity of community colleges and HSIs to educate Latinas and Latinos in STEM fields."[59]

Conclusion

This chapter has shown that there are large gaps in the participation of three important groups in U.S. engineering. Despite representing nearly half of the U.S. labor force, women comprise just 13% of employed engineers and 18% of new bachelor's-degreed engineers entering the labor force each year. African Americans and Hispanics are also significantly underrepresented in engineering, at only 5% and 6% of the workforce, respectively. White males continue to be the largest population group in engineering and among engineering bachelor's degree recipients. In 2010 the 40,128 bachelor's degrees in engineering awarded to this group represented 57% of all engineering and 8% of all bachelor's degrees earned by white males. If African American males, Hispanic males and U.S. citizen and permanent resident females of all racial/ethnic backgrounds earned bachelor's degrees at the same rate as did white males – assuming the overall number of bachelor's degrees remained unchanged – then an additional 68,000 U.S. citizens and permanent residents would have earned bachelor's degrees in engineering in 2010, or nearly twice the current number.[60] In short, by merely tapping the talent in the United States and increasing the factual information that young people, parents, and teachers have about the work of engineers, our nation would be able to meet the stated demand for engineering talent.

As Margaret Loftus states, "unless we can make engineering a whole lot more appealing to all under-represented minorities, the United States stands to lose its position in the world as a technological innovator."[61] We have suggested a number of strategies that may alleviate the persistent gap in high school preparation of Latinos and African Americans in order to provide members of these groups with real access to engineering. Better messaging about engineering is likely to provide a stronger attraction for women.

Community colleges can serve a critical role in addressing the on-going disparities in high school preparation of Latinos and African Americans. They are also critical in providing opportunities for career-changers in our technologically-driven society to retool their skills to fit into openings in engineering and other STEM fields. Likewise, the community colleges can serve as a bridge to well-paying jobs for our veterans who have served the country.

References

1. Zax, D. (2008). Up Close: Goal Oriented. *Prism*, p. 27. Retrieved from <http://www.prism-magazine.org/sept08/upclose.cfm>
2. In this study we use the terms Latino and Hispanic interchangeably. Whenever the terms "White", "African American" or "Black" are used, it is implied that these refer to non-Hispanic-descent individuals within those groups, consistent with common practice in reporting.
3. Frehill, L.M. (2010). *Fact Sheet: U.S. Engineering Work Force* White Plains, NY: NACME, Inc. Note: "All engineering occupations" includes "engineering managers", "engineers", "engineering technicians," and "sales engineers."
4. The evidence suggests, however, that Asian-Americans have experienced some negative impacts associated with minority status in professional fields like engineering.

5. National Science Foundation, National Center for Science and Engineering Statistics (2011). *Women, Minorities, and Persons with Disabilities in Science and Engineering.* NSF 11-09, Arlington VA, Table 1-3.

6. Slaughter, J. (2007). *A Focus on Diversity: an Agenda Item for the 2008 Presidential Campaign.* National Action Council for Minorities in Engineering (NACME). Retrieved from <http://www.eweek.org/site/About/diversity_NACME_keynote.shtml>

7. Ibid.

8. Aud, S., Fox, M.A., and KewalRamani, A. (2010). *Status and Trends in the Education of Racial and Ethnic Groups.* IES National Center for Education Statistics, p. iii.

9. National Science Foundation (2012). *Science and Engineering Indicators, 2012*, (NSB 12-01), Arlington, VA., Chapter 3.

10. Computation based on 8.4% of 930,713 total bachelor's degrees awarded to female U.S. citizens and permanent residents in 2010. Actual number of engineering bachelor's degrees awarded to this group was 12,766: $(930,713 * .084) - 12,766 = 65,812$.

11. U.S. Census (2012). "U.S. Census, Facts and Figures". Retrieved from <http://www.census.gov/newsroom/releases/archives/facts_for_features_special_editions/cb12-ff05.html>

12. Ibid.

13. U.S. Census (2011). *Women in the Workforce.* Retrieved from <http://www.census.gov/newsroom/pdf/women_workforce_slides.pdf>

14. Frehill, L.M. (1997) Education and Occupational Sex Segregation: The Decision to Major in Engineering. *Sociological Quarterly*, 38(2). And Frehill, LM. (1993). *Education and Occupational Sex Segregation: The Case of Women in Engineering.* (Tucson, AZ: Doctoral Dissertation),

15. Consentino de Cohen, C. (2009). Retention is not the problem. *Prism*, October, p. 55. Retrieved from <http://www.prism-magazine.org/oct09/tt_02.cfm>

16. National Academy of Engineering (2008). *Changing the Conversation: Messages for Improving the Public Understanding of Engineering* (Washington, DC: National Academies Press), and Eccles, J.S. (2007). "Where are all the women? Gender differences in participation in physical science and engineering", pp. 199-210 in Ceci, S.J. and Williams, W.M. (2007). *Why Aren't More Women in Science? Top Researchers Debate the Evidence.* (Washington, DC: American Psychological Association).

17. Eccles, J.S. (2007) Where are all the women? Gender differences in participation in physical science and engineering. pp. 199-210 in Ceci, S.J. and Williams, W.M., *Why Aren't More Women in Science? Top Researchers Debate the Evidence*. (Washington, DC: American Psychological Association); Frehill, L.M. (1997). Education and occupational sex segregation: The decision to major in engineering. *Sociological Quarterly 38*(2), 1997, and Sax, LJ and Harper, CE. (2005). *Origins of the Gender Gap: Pre-College and College Influences on Differences Between Men and Women*, paper presented at the Association for Institutional Research, San Diego, CA.

18. Correll, S.J. (2004). Constraints into Preferences: Gender, Status and Emerging Career Aspirations. *American Sociological Review* 69(1): 93-113. And Cech, E., Rubineau, B., Silbey, S. and Seron, C. (2011). Professional role confidence and gendered persistence in engineering. *American Sociological Review* 76(5): 641-666.

19. National Academy of Engineering. Committee on Public Understanding of Engineering Messages (2008). *Changing the Conversation: Messages for Improving Public Understanding of Engineering*. National Academy Press.

20. The mean length of time to earn an engineering doctoral degree was 7.3 years for the 2010 temporary resident engineering doctoral degree recipients, according to the National Science Foundation's annual *Science and Engineering Doctorates, 2010*. U.S. citizens and permanent residents who earned engineering doctoral degrees spent a median 6.3 years in graduate school to earn their Ph.D.

21. The National Science Foundation estimates of the S&E workforce in the volume "Science and Engineering Indicators, 2012" are based on analyses of the Scientists and Engineers Statistical Analysis System (SESTAT) database, the population for which are predominantly individuals with S&E bachelor's degrees. Estimates of the S&E workforce using Bureau of Labor Statistics data from the Current Population Survey or the American Community Survey differ from those of the NSF's SESTAT because individuals of all educational levels are included and because there are many technician occupations included in the broad categories of the BLS Standard Occupational Code (SOC).

22. National Science Foundation (2012). *Science and Engineering Indicators, 2012*, NSB 12-01, Arlington, VA., Chapter 3.

23. Frehill, L. (2012). Gender and Career Outcomes of U.S. Engineers. *International Journal of Gender, Science And Technology, 4(2)*. Retrieved from <http://genderandset.open.ac.uk/index.php/genderandset/article/view /199>

24. Fouad, N.A., Singh, R. (2011). *Stemming the Tide: Why Women Leave Engineering.* University of Wisconsin-Milwaukee.
25. Pritchard, C. (2007). Gender Gap: Diversity Down Under. *Prism*, Summer 2007, 16(9).
26. Pourrat, Y. (project coordinator). (2005). *Women: Creating Cultures of Success for Women Engineers: Synthesis Report.* Retrieved from: <http://www.womeng.net/intro.htm>. Mills, J., et al. (2008) *An update on women's progress in the Australian engineering workforce.* Barton ACT: Engineers Australia. Retrieved from <http://www.engineersaustralia.org.au/shadomx/apps/fms/fmsdownload.cfm?file_uuid=7DA323DA-E3CC-A6FB-8DB3-4D97EFFBBEEF&siteName=ieaust>; ENSC/CEDIS (2008). *Deliverable No 20: Periodic Progress Report on WP7 results Transversal integrating analysis and interpretation*, PROMETEA: Empowering Women Engineers in Industrial and Academic Research. Retrieved from: http://www.prometea.info/. Fouad, N. A. and Singh, R. (2011). *Stemming the Tide: Why Women Leave Engineering.* University of Wisconsin-Milwaukee. And Frehill, LM. (2012). Gender and Career Outcomes of U.S. Engineers. *International Journal of Gender, Science and Technology,* 4(2). Retrieved October 21, 2012 from <http://genderandset.open.ac.uk/index.php/genderandset/article/view/199>
27. National Science Foundation (2012). *Science and Engineering Indicators, 2012*, National Science Foundation, NSB 12-01, Arlington, VA, p. 3-40.
28. Report of the Congressional Commission on the Advancement of Women and Minorities in Science, Engineering and Technology Development. (2000). *Land of Plenty: Diversity as America's Competitive Edge in Science, Engineering and Technology*, September 2000. Retrieved from <http://www.nsf.gov/pubs/2000/cawmset0409/cawmset_0409.pdf>
29. Fouad, N.A. and Singh, R. (2011). Women in Engineering 2011 Report. *Stemming the Tide: Why Women Leave Engineering.* University of Wisconsin-Milwaukee. Retrieved from <http://files.campus.edublogs.org/www5.uwm.edu/dist/a/4/files/2011/03/NSF_Women-Executive-Summary-0314.pdf>
30. Holmes, A. (2011). Technically, Science Fields Must Be Made Less Lonely for Women. *Washington Post*, 23 September 2011, p. C3.
31. Hill, C., Corbett, C., and St. Rose, A. (2010). American Association of University Women Report. *Why So Few? Women in Science, Technology, Engineering and Mathematics*, February 2010.

32. Hewlett, S.A., Luck, C.B., Servon, L.J., Sherbinm L., Shiller, P., Sosnovich, E., and Sumberg, K. (2008). The Athena Factor: Reversing the Brain Drain in Science, Engineering, and Technology. *Harvard Business Review*, May 2008.

33. Frehill, L.M. (2012). Gender and Career Outcomes of U.S. Engineers. *International Journal of Gender, Science and Technology,* 4(2). Retrieved 21 October 2012 from <http://genderandset.open.ac.uk/index.php/genderandset/article/view/199>

34. As mentioned earlier, we will use the terms Latino and Hispanic interchangeably. We recognize that there are significant differences within this large and growing category of the U.S. population due to immigrant status, country of origin, and socioeconomic status and that these can impact participation in engineering. For more detail about how the U.S. Latino population participates in engineering, please see a 2008 report by the National Action Council on Minorities in Engineering, Inc. (NACME, Inc.) "The New American Dilemma: A Data-Based Look at Diversity."

35. Hewlett, S.A., Luck, C.B., Servon, L.J., Sherbinm L., Shiller, P., Sosnovich, E., Sumberg, K. (2008). The Athena Factor: Reversing the Brain Drain in Science, Engineering, and Technology. *Harvard Business Review*, May 2008.

36. Source: author's analysis of U.S. Census Bureau. 2010. "American Community Survey 2009" PUMS datafile.

37. Overall, these same three groups accounted for 12.5% of all engineering bachelor's degrees, based on author's analysis of Integrated Postsecondary Education Data System (IPEDS) accessed using the NSF WebCASPAR database system.

38. The three fields, engineering, engineering technology and computer science, were combined because the relative sample size within the BPS data was small: aggregation was necessary to permit the computations shown here.

39. Sieff, K. (2011). Closing 'The Gifted Gap'. *Washington Post*, 7 November 2011, p. A7.

40. Bowen, W.G., Chingos, M.M., and McPherson, M.S. (2009). *Crossing the Finish Line: Completing College at America's Public Universities*. Princeton, NJ: Princeton University Press.

41. Barahmpour, T. (2010). Study: Md., Va. Latino Kids Fare Better than Peers Elsewhere, Still Face Hurdles. *Washington Post*, 29 April 2010.

42. Loftus, M. (2006). A Future Engineer? *Prism*, December 2006. Retrieved from <http://www.prism-magazine.org/dec06/feature_future.cfm>

43. Santiago, D.A. (2008). *Modeling Hispanic-Serving Institutions (HSIs): Campus Practices that Work for Latino Students.* ¡Excelencia! in Education, Washington DC.

44. Santiago, D.A. (2007). *Choosing Hispanic-Serving Institutions (HSIs): A Closer Look at Latino Students' College Choices.* ¡Excelencia! in Education, Washington, DC.

45. Loftus, M. (2008). Untapped Potential. *Prism*, October 2008. Retrieved from <http://www.prism-magazine.org/oct08/feature_03.cfm>.

46. National Action Council for Minorities in Engineering (2011). Data Deck.

47. Feagin, J., Vera, H., and Imani, N. (1996). *The Agony of Education: Black Students at a White University.* Routledge.

48. National Science Foundation. (2012) *Science and Engineering Indicators, 2012: Science and Engineering Labor Force*, January 2012, Table 3-26.

49. González y Musielak, D.E. (2002). Missing Part of the Equation. *Hispanic Business Magazine*, July 2002. Retrieved from <http://www.hispanicbusiness.com/2002/7/31/missing_part_of_the_equation.htm>

50. Caranza, R. (1999). "Minorities in the Engineering Workplace: Overcoming Barriers to Success". Retrieved from <http://www.graduatingengineer.com/articles/19990915/Minorities-in-the-Engineering-Workplace:-Overcoming-Barriers-to-Success>

51. Feagin, J., Vera, H., and Imani, N. (1996). *The Agony of Education: Black Students at a White University.* Routledge.

52. Loftus, M. (2009). Flight to Achievement. *Prism*, April 2009. Retrieved from <http://www.prism-magazine.org/apr09/feature_01.cfm>

53. Ibid.

54. National Math and Science Initiative (2012). Retrieved from <http://www.nationalmathandscience.org/sites/default/files/resource/NMSI%20one-pager%2001-13-12.pdf>

55. The numbers of undergraduates enrolled at the A. James Clark School of Engineering and within the Department of Mechanical Engineering at the University of Maryland, College Park, were obtained through the University's Office of Institutional Research Planning and Assessment (IRPA). IRPA tracks institutional data for the University of Maryland for both internal and external sources, using nationally accepted definitions. Numbers were gathered and calculated from fall semester University status reports for the years 2000 through 2010, along with breakdowns of both race and gender.

56. Dowd, A., Malcom, L., and Macias, E. (2010). *Improving Transfer Access to STEM Bachelor's Degrees at Hispanic Serving Institutions through the America COMPETES Act*, March 2010, p. 6. USC Rossier School of Education.

57. Mattis, M.C. and Sislin, J. (2005). *Enhancing the Community College Pathway to Engineering Careers.* Washington, DC: National Academies Press.

58. Rivera, E. (2010). *Community College Transfers in Baccalaureate Engineering Degree Programs*, White Plains, NY: NACME, Inc. Retrieved from <http://www.nacme.org/user/docs/CCTS-%20complete.pdf>, accessed 29 October 2012.

59. Dowd, A., Malcom, L., and Macias, E. (2010). *Improving Transfer Access to STEM Bachelor's Degrees at Hispanic Serving Institutions through the America COMPETES Act*, March 2010, p. 3. USC Rossier School of Education.

60. Computation was performed by multiplying the number of bachelor's degrees earned by each of the three groups under consideration – all women (930,713 bachelor's), Black men (51,969 bachelor's), and Hispanic men (57,416 bachelor's) – by 8.4%, engineering degrees as a percentage of all bachelor's degrees earned by White males. This produced an estimated expected 87,702 bachelor's degrees in engineer versus the actual 19,645 bachelor's degrees in engineering earned by these three underrepresented groups. 87,702 – 19,645 = 68,057 additional bachelor's degrees.

61. Loftus, M. (2006). A Future Engineer?. *Prism*, December 2006. Retrieved from <http://www.prism-magazine.org/dec06/feature_future.cfm>

Chapter 5

Globalization

This is a new world and it is not America-centric. The new world has aggressive R&D and educational budgets with a growing S&T population. The central question for us is – how will we manage our policies to take advantage of this new reality.

The issues of culture, immigration and groups underrepresented in STEM not only play an important role in the development of the engineering workforce in the country, but they have also received a fair amount of direct attention in how national policies, which affect the supply and demand of S&E professionals are shaped. The issue of globalization of the S&E workforce, which plays a powerful role in the education and movement of S&E professionals worldwide have received much generalized press, has not leant itself easily to a coherent national strategy addressing this extremely important phenomena.

The challenge of developing enough quality S&E talent domestically is not an issue facing only the U.S. An article in *The Economist* on the global talent shortage summarized the situation by noting that:

"rich countries have progressed from simply relaxing their immigration laws to actively luring highly qualified people … India and China are trying to entice back some of their brightest people from abroad. Singapore's Ministry of Manpower even has an international talent division … Germany has made it easier for workers to get visas. Britain has offered more work permits for skilled migrants. France has introduced a 'scientist visa' … Ireland's government works hard to recruit overseas talent … Singapore … is going out of its way to import foreign talent."[1]

Within the global competition for talent, engineers as innovators could play an increasingly important role. Countries that properly cultivate and nurture their engineering community will have a tremendous advantage from both and economic and national security perspective. Most developing countries are in the process of building infrastructure—education, energy, communications and transportation systems—that present challenges across the globe because of natural resources limitations. Hence, the engineering advancements in these countries will contribute to a much larger body of work upon which engineers the world-over will be able to innovate. Thus, the country which properly nourishes and cultivates its engineering community will have a tremendous economic and national security advantage.

Even as we have a perceived shortage of engineers in the U.S., engineers are leaving to work in Bangalore, Hong Kong, Africa, and many other countries, lured by increasing numbers of overseas positions that are said to offer a variety of attractive opportunities such as higher total compensation packages and the ability to travel.[2] Will engineers become a commodity? Will they simply go where the money and working conditions are best, and where there is challenge and excitement?

At the same time, however, it has become clear that as the world has become flatter, international engagement for scientists and engineers is paramount to ensuring that these professionals are able to stay on the cutting edge of research and innovation. The National Science Board notes that growing international science and engineering expertise, "presents definite challenges to U.S. competitiveness in high technology areas, and to its position as a world leader."[3] In short, having U.S. scientists and engineers engaging with their international peers needs to be a focus of national policy makers in the next 10 years. Further, despite the many barriers that currently exist, international engagement is especially important for those who work for the Department of Defense.

Global S&E Labor Force

Significant growth of the global S&E community over the past 30 years has been fueled by rapid growth in communication networks, political changes (e.g., the breakups of the USSR and Yugoslavia, the end of Apartheid in South Africa, and the "opening" of China to multinational corporations), developing economies, increased government investment in R&D, increased access to and quality of education, and the growth of worldwide R&D expenditures. While the U.S. and Europe traditionally employed the majority of S&Es, developing economies such as India, China, South Korea and others have now developed significant R&D and educational facilities.[4] Figure 5.1, illustrates growth in S&E research personnel from 1995 to 2009Until 2003 U.S., Chinese and European Union (EU) growth was strong; since then, growth in China, South Korea, and the EU have been strong while the U.S., Japan and Russia have remained relatively stagnant. The NSF has noted that "increased global S&E capacity offers great opportunities for scientific advancement and cross-border scientific cooperation. It offers a larger pool of researchers for both U.S. public and private enterprises, and a wider range of possibilities for collaborations and utilization of major foreign research facilities."[5]

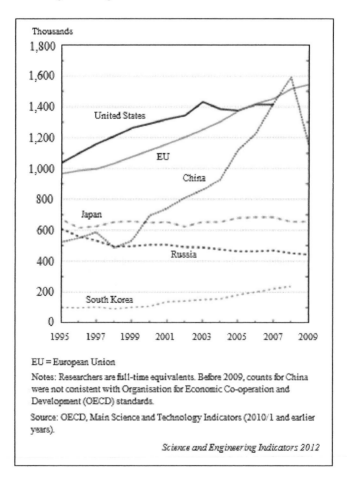

EU = European Union

Notes: Researchers are full-time equivalents. Before 2009, counts for China were not conistent with Organisation for Economic Co-operation and Development (OECD) standards.

Source: OECD, Main Science and Technology Indicators (2010/1 and earlier years).

Science and Engineering Indicators 2012

Figure 5.1: Estimated Number of Researchers in Selected Countries/Regions: 1995-2009[6]

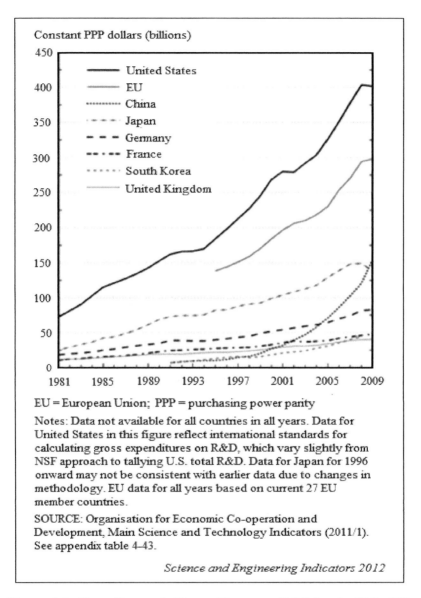

Figure 5.2: Gross Domestic Expenditures on R&D by the U.S., EU, and Other Selected Countries, 1981-2009

There is little directly comparable data available on the global S&E labor force.[7] Using the best data that are available, and with the caveat that comparability is an issue, it is clear that global expenditures in R&D have grown significantly over the past 30 years. The U.S. grew at an average of 5% from 1999 to 2009, and still led global R&D expenditures at 31% of the global total in 2009, down from 38% in 1999. The most notable growth shown in Figure 5.2 was China, which has had exponential growth n R&D expenditures since 2001.[8] Likewise, R&D growth in other Asian countries has been rapid over the past 30 years, with Asian countries accounting for 24% of global R&D expenditures in 1999 and growing to, 32% by 2009. During this ten-year period, China's growth was 20%, or four times that of the U.S. while South Korea averaged nearly 10% growth, or double that of the U.S.. In contrast, Japan's R&D growth was much more modest: at just 4%, Japan's R&D growth was about 20% less than the U.S.[9]

R&D intensity, computed as the ratio of R&D expenditures over GDP (expressed as a percentage), is another metric used for international comparisons. For the U.S., since 1999 R&D intensity fluctuated between 2.6% to 2.8% and was at 2.9% in 2009. A number of other nations surpassed the U.S. in R&D intensity: Israel, Sweden, Finland, Japan, South Korea, Switzerland, and Taiwan, reflecting the important role of technological innovation in these nations as economic engines. While China's R&D intensity is relatively low at 1.7%, this has doubled since 1999.[10]

R&D expenditures by U.S. companies overseas have also grown tremendously. From 1997 to 2008 the share of R&D performed by U.S. majority-owned affiliates in Asia (other than Japan) more than doubled, including increases in the share performed in China, South Korea, Singapore, and India.[11] Multinational corporations, including those based in the United States, have expanded research operations to locate in emerging product markets and in areas where world-class S&E talent is located.

Migration and Virtual Migration

Our flattening world has resulted in significant growth of high skill migration of technical talent. Although internationally comparable data on S&E migration does not exist,[12] there is agreement that the world is becoming more educated, and that levels of high skill migration have been increasing over recent decades, particularly to OECD countries.[13] Docquier and Rapoport reported that "the number of highly educated immigrants living in the OECD member countries increased by 70% during the 1990s (and doubled for those originating from developing countries) against a 30% increase for low-skill immigrants."[14] OECD data are likely the best available indicator of overall high skill migration; as Docquier and Rapoport further estimate that immigration to OECD countries represents 85% of global high skill migration.[15] This migration is facilitated by new and more aggressive immigration policies. In the United States, the Immigration Act of 1990 was far ahead of the more recent immigration reforms in other countries. The 190 Act more than doubled employment-based visas, making 140,000 visas available with an emphasis on high skilled migrants to the U.S. The Act also established the H-1B visa program to provide another mechanism for foreign workers with special skills to enter the United States. Though initially capped at 65,000, the American Competitive and Workforce Improvement Act of 1998 raised this cap to 115,000 in 1999 and 2000, dropped to 107,500 in 2001 and back to 65,000 in 2002. Another act, the American Competitiveness in the Twenty-First Century Act of 2000, increased the number of H-1B visas to 195,000 for FY 2001, 2002, and 2003. The H-1B Visa Reform Act of 2004 enabled 20,000 more visas for individuals who had earned a master's degree or higher from a U.S. college or university. As of November 2012, a number of other measures are making their way through either the House or the Senate, which would further increase the accessibility of visas for those who are in high-skilled STEM occupations or for immigrant entrepreneurs. With the recent economic downturn, however, whereas the lottery for H-1B visas was oversubscribed in the early years of the 21st century, in the past three years, the program has not reached the cap.[16]

As previously noted in Chapter 3, Australia, Germany and Canada and other countries have also changed their immigration processes to attract skilled workers in areas of need. Bartlett notes that "Finland, Ireland, Portugal, Spain, Sweden, and the United Kingdom-have revoked the EU's seven-year ban on the entry of guest workers from recently admitted East European states."[17] Asian economies such as Singapore, Taiwan and China have implemented incentives to lure highly-skilled doctoral scientists and engineers as they grow national R&D capacity and build world-class university research programs.

The globalization of higher education has continued to expand. Although the United States continues to attract the largest number and proportion of foreign students worldwide, its share of foreign students has decreased in recent years. Universities in several other countries (e.g., Canada, Japan, and the United Kingdom) have expanded their enrollment of foreign S&E students.[18] With more favorable immigration policies than those found in the U.S., these students have an opportunity to stay in their host country, and this directly impacts our ability to attract talented S&Es to the U.S.

Besides physical migration there is now 'virtual migration' or teaming, where workers increasingly engage with their counterparts in foreign countries. An international collaboration module in the NSF's 2006 Scientists and Engineers Statistical Analysis System (SESTAT[19]) asked U.S. S&Es if they had engaged with workers in other countries during the survey reference week. The results illustrate in 2006, U.S. S&Es were interacting globally on a regular basis.[20]

- Workers in S&E occupations had much higher rates of international engagement (28%) than those in non-S&E (16%) or S&E-related (8%) occupations.
- Among those in S&E occupations, computer and mathematical scientists and engineers had the highest rates of international engagement and social scientists had the lowest rates.
- Doctorate holders had substantially higher rates of international engagement than individuals whose highest degrees were at the master's or bachelor's level. Professional degree holders had the lowest rates of all.
- Foreign-born survey respondents (24%) reported international engagement more often than U.S.-born individuals (15%).
- Those who earned degrees both in the United States and abroad had the highest rates of international engagement (31%). The comparable figure for those who earned their degrees abroad was 23%, and for those with only U.S. degrees it was 16%.

Due to constant improvements in tools, technologies and methodologies, the way modern engineering work is performed has changed. Now an engineer can communicate with global teams instantly over the Internet, work effectively in virtual teams across time zones, employ virtual design and simulation tools in tandem with other locations around the world, and access vast digital information resources. Thus, engineering has been transformed into a global and 'outsourceable' endeavor. With new digital measurement and simulation capabilities, in many cases an engineer can be anywhere in the world and successfully design a system without physical access to where the system may be utilized. Unlike other careers, such as being surgeon, chef, or trial lawyer, engineering is no longer a career that is 'sticky' (i.e., a job that requires some level of physical presence to be performed).

There are numerous examples of truly global engineering projects that utilize virtual teams of employees across time and space barriers. General Motors (GM), Ford and others have 'world' vehicles both on sale and in development – a single vehicle designed to be sold across global markets served by the companies. R&D, design and manufacturing teams from multiple countries work together on not just standard product development but also incorporate relevant regional requirements into vehicle design. Increasingly global engineering teams serve multiple global regions. For example, in late 2012 GM began production of a vehicle for the Indian market that was designed by SAIC Motor, GM's Chinese partner.[21] Corning Display Technologies, a premiere developer of glass products for LCDs, built a team with engineers from the U.S., Japan and Taiwan to develop LCD glass finishing and processes.[22] Technologies for the world's largest commercial aircraft, the Airbus A380, were conceived by four globally disparate teams, all divisions of the parent company, European Aeronautic Defence and Space Company (EADS). Boeing's 787 Dreamliner aircraft was developed by groups from France, Japan, Germany, Canada, Italy, Australia, the United States and Korea. The frequency of these transnational engineering projects has risen significantly as more countries scale up the quality and size of their own R&D infrastructure, and as more companies extend their R&D presence to other countries. Companies have found success by implementing the same tools, technologies and processes in new R&D centers as those used by their groups in the U.S. and other home countries.

The international migration of S&E talent and teaming between S&E

> *"Singapore-this may be a small country, but when it comes to research and development, it's thinking big. Witness Fusionopolis, a trio of gleaming, high-rise towers housing state-of-the-art labs for 2,400 scientists and engineers – plus offices a gym, restaurants, shops, a theater, and three floors of posh loft apartments."[23]*

researchers across the globe as a result of global R&D infrastructure development outside the U.S. has effected a rise in the level of international co-authorship of S&E journal articles. Figure 5.3 illustrates the growth of international co-authorship both from the U.S. and other countries from 1990 to 2010. In 2000 23% of U.S. articles were internationally coauthored, which increased to 32% in 2010. Not surprisingly, though, international co-authorship is even more common in the European Union, where international collaboration has been incentivized by large Framework Research Programs. International co-authorship has increased in Japan and among the Asia-8, with half of some nations' journal articles having authors from more than one nation.[24]

Table 5.1: S&E Article Output Rankings by S&E Field, 1995 and 2005[25]

Country/Economy	All fields 1995	All fields 2005	Engineering 1995	Engineering 2005	Chemistry 1995	Chemistry 2005	Physics 1995	Physics 2005	Geosciences 1995	Geosciences 2005	Mathematics 1995	Mathematics 2005	Biological Sciences 1995	Biological Sciences 2005	Medical Sciences 1995	Medical Sciences 2005
U.S.	1	1	1	1	1	1	1	2	1	1	1	1	1	1	1	1
Japan	2	2	2	3	2	3	2	2	5	3	8	7	3	2	3	3
United Kingdom	3	3	3	5	6	8	6	7	2	2	4	5	2	3	2	2
Germany	4	4	4	6	3	4	3	4	6	5	3	4	4	4	4	4
China	14	5	8	2	11	2	7	3	15	7	9	3	20	7	21	11
France	5	6	6	7	5	6	5	5	4	6	2	2	5	5	5	7
Canada	6	7	5	8	10	12	9	12	3	4	5	10	6	6	7	6
Italy	8	8	10	10	8	10	8	8	9	9	6	6	7	8	6	5
Spain	11	9	15	12	9	9	11	11	11	10	10	8	11	9	11	10
South Korea	22	10	13	4	15	11	15	9	35	19	24	12	29	13	31	14
Australia	9	11	12	14	14	17	17	18	7	8	11	13	8	10	9	9
India	12	12	9	11	7	7	10	10	13	12	17	21	14	12	19	20
Russia	7	13	7	13	4	5	4	6	8	11	7	9	9	18	22	28
Netherlands	10	14	14	18	13	16	14	17	10	13	13	16	10	11	8	8
Taiwan	18	15	11	9	17	14	20	13	23	15	20	20	22	19	20	16
Sweden	13	16	16	19	18	21	18	19	12	18	15	18	12	14	10	12
Brazil	23	17	25	16	25	15	21	15	24	16	19	15	19	15	24	17
Switzerland	15	18	19	21	16	18	13	16	16	14	16	19	13	16	12	15
Turkey	34	19	26	17	29	20	37	25	29	21	44	27	34	24	25	13
Poland	19	20	18	20	12	13	12	14	27	29	14	14	25	23	28	26

Notes: Countries initially ranked on 2005 total article output. Article counts from set of journals covered by Science Citation Index (SCI) and Social Sciences Citation Index (SSCI). Articles classified by year of publication and assigned to country/economy on basis of institutional address(es) listed in article. Articles on fractional-count basis, i.e. for articles with collaboration institutions from multiple countries/economies, each country/economy receives fractional credit on basis of proportion of its participating institutions, China includes Hong Kong.
Sources: Thomson Scientific, SCI and SSCI, http://scientific.thomson.com/products/categories/citation; ipIQ, Inc.; and National Science Foundation, Division of Science Resources Statistics, special tabulations. Science and Engineering Indicators 2008

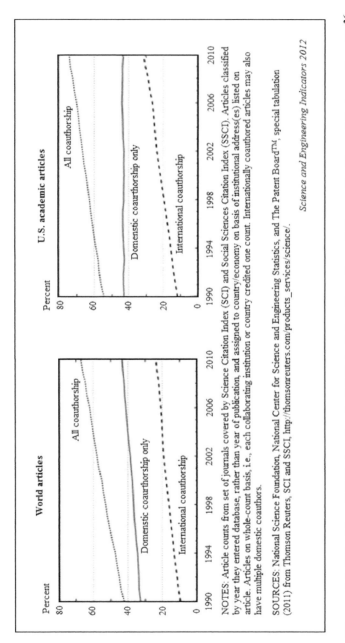

NOTES: Article counts from set of journals covered by Science Citation Index (SCI) and Social Sciences Citation Index (SSCI). Articles classified by year they entered database, rather than year of publication, and assigned to country/economy on basis of institutional address(es) listed on article. Articles on whole-count basis, i.e., each collaborating institution or country credited one count. Internationally coauthored articles may also have multiple domestic coauthors.

SOURCES: National Science Foundation, National Center for Science and Engineering Statistics, and The Patent Board™, special tabulation (2011) from Thomson Reuters, SCI and SSCI, http://thomsonreuters.com/products_services/science/.

Science and Engineering Indicators 2012

Figure 5.3: World and U.S. Academic S&E Articles Coauthored Domestically and Internationally[26]

The data in Table 5.1 shows trends in S&E article output from 1995 to 2005, another international indicator of R&D output. Within the category of engineering, the U.S. retained 1st place from 1995 to 2005. China moved from 8th to 2nd, South Korea went from 13th to 4th, and Taiwan climbed from 11th to 9th, reflecting a growing challenge to U.S. R&D superiority. Meanwhile, however, India moved from 9th to 11th, perhaps reflecting the difficult quality issues the country faces with engineering education, which is highly privatized.

Engineering Education

Widespread access to, as well as the quality of, engineering education has major implications for the employable global S&E workforce. For example, the McKinsey Global Institute found that with regards to the number of available professionals, India alone had nearly as many young professional engineers as the United States, and China had more than twice as many.[27] They also found, however, that while 50% of engineers in Poland or Hungary were suitable for work in multinational companies, only 10% of Chinese and 25% of Indians would be suitable, noting that "in India the overall quality of the educational system, apart from the top universities, could improve significantly."[28] The report went on to encourage countries to improve the quality of their graduates, rather than simply creating greater quantities of graduating students. Indian companies have found that graduates of lower-tier engineering programs still lack critical skills, and, as a result, are investing heavily in three-month, six-month, nine-month, or even one-year training courses, and are setting up university-like facilities for the purposes of retraining their own employees. As seen by the growth of companies such as India's Infosys and Tata Consultancy Services, this approach has been very successful.

Statistics such as the tertiary attendance, number of engineering colleges, and size of the S&E educational infrastructure for countries like India and China show a recent rate of growth far beyond that of the U.S.[29] Also, while science and engineering educational and professional research infrastructures are improving rapidly within these countries, the quality of the graduates from their universities is not necessarily keeping pace. An examination of the 2011 data for Engineering/Technology and Computer Sciences from the Academic Ranking of World Universities (ARWU)[30] found that the U.S. ranked 32 of its universities amongst the top 50 in the world while China had five, and India had none. The rankings of institutions within these countries are improving, however, largely due to increased cooperative activities with highly ranked institutions from other countries.

"India needs to recruit at least one million new faculty members for its college and universities if it is to meet the government's ambitious target to offer a higher education (HE) place to 20% of all young people by 2020. The number of PhDs being produced by the current Indian HE system falls far short of meeting this need. The most promising way to fill this gap is to recruit back many of the over 100,000 Indians who are studying in the US each year to obtain a graduate degree and the many others who are studying in other nations or who have completed their degrees and begun academic careers abroad."[31]

A new comparative index developed recently by The Boston Consulting Group to evaluate the global competitiveness of educational systems is shown in Table 5.2. This table shows that when examining the list of the top 10 countries, China has a strong showing at 3rd place, and India is in 5th place. When looking at individual measures, however, it becomes clear that high scores for India and China are based on extraordinarily high enrollment numbers (3-4x U.S. numbers) rather than a strong performance in the area of overall quality. In the "Engineering Grads" category, measured by the number of qualified engineers entering the workforce, China and India score approximately one-tenth as high as the U.S., U.K., Germany, France and Canada, nations with high-quality, well-established engineering colleges. Similarly both India and China score poorly in the "Elite University" category. India also scores very poorly in the "Expenditure" category-as mentioned in Chapter 2, India's public education system lags that of many nations, so the private sector has expanded to meet labor market needs.

While India and China have a significant amount of work ahead of them to challenge U.S. educational strength as characterized by this measure, the large populations competing for a small number of spaces in the best institutions as a means to secure a profitable career underlie the elevation of engineering and scholastic skills within those nations noted in Chapter 2. In other words: in advanced economies such as the United States in which there are many avenues to prosperity for young people, some of those young people will choose to dedicate their effort to science, mathematics and engineering, while others will pursue the arts, entertainment, medicine, or any of a plethora of other fields with different skill requirements. But even as the economies of India and

China grow and diversify, the sheer size of their youth populations will likely provide abundant raw material ready to take advantage of the educational institutions that are able to survive the "growth spurt" currently underway in those nations.

Education Strength					
Which countries have the most competitive educational systems world-wide? The Boston Consulting Group's new E4 index assigns points in four categories, each equally weighted in the final score. Of the 20 countries ranked, here are the top 10.					
Country	Total Points	Enrollment Points	Expenditure Points	Engineering Grads Points	Elite University Points
U.S.	237	25	73	48	91
U.K.	125	4	26	46	48
China	115	86	17	4	8
Germany	104	5	25	37	38
India	104	90	4	3	6
France	87	4	24	41	18
Canada	85	2	25	39	18
Japan	72	7	31	19	16
Brazil	38	17	16	2	3
Russia	32	9	10	10	3

Table 5.2: Boston Consulting Group's E4 Index of Education Strength[32]

In recent years, U.S. colleges and universities have been expanding their international reach by entering into agreements to build either joint or branch campuses with universities in India, China and others. As of 2006, Western universities operated 1,300 joint programs in China. Since then a significant number of institutions have developed international branch campuses or forged other operating agreements. The Observatory on Borderless Higher Education reported the development of 162 global branch campuses as of 2009, an increase of 43% over the previous three years, with almost all campuses established by Western universities[33], with American universities accounting for 48 percent.[34] As of October 2012, the Cross-Border Education Research Team (C-BERT) reported 169 active global branch campuses spread throughout the world (see Figure 5.4).[35,36]

Examples of U.S. University Joint Ventures with Foreign Institutions

- Stanford – operates a research and education center in China's Peking University
- University of California, Berkeley – developing plans to open a large research and teaching facility in Shanghai
- Georgia Tech – operates campuses in Singapore and France, research facilities in Ireland and Costa Rica, and has dual-degree options in Shanghai
- Texas A&M offering degrees at a branch campus in Doha, Qatar
- New York University has created a branch campus in Abu Dhabi, UAE
- Johns Hopkins has had a program in place with Nanjing University in China for 20 years
- The State University of New York-Stony Brook has a dual-degree partnership with Nanjing University
- Rochester Institute of Technology has a microelectronics program in Dubai

Examples of Non-U.S. University Multinational Ventures

- France: Université Paris-Sorbonne Abu Dhabi (UPSAD) has been set up in the UAE
- Australia: Monash University has a campus in South Africa
- Australia: Australian Royal Melbourne Institute of Technology has campuses in Hanoi and Ho Chi Minh City
- Scotland: Heriot-Watt University has a campus in Dubai
- Scotland: Queen Margaret University has a branch in Singapore
- UK: University of Nottingham has a branch campus in Ningbo, China and one in Malaysia

The new partnerships and locations of major educational institutions are actively being incentivized by other countries. India's Minister for Human Resource Development has been working to open India's heavily regulated educational system[37] so that Indian students could get a U.S. education in India at a lower cost than travelling to the U.S. In June 2012, India's University Grants Commission approved the country's most highly-accredited institutions to enter into dual-degree programs with "top 500" foreign educational institutions in an effort to provide top quality education from foreign providers to Indian students.[38]

Figure 5.4: Locations of International Branch Campuses[39]

Education City, in Doha, Qatar, is a 14 square kilometer experiment to bring an American education to the Gulf, with six U.S. educational institutions involved: Texas A&M University, Cornell University, Northwestern University, Carnegie Mellon University, Georgetown University and Virginia Commonwealth University, as well as one French (HEC Paris) and one U.K. (UCL). The quality and global recognition goals for this project are high – there is a requirement that each Education City institution give out degrees identical to those received at their home institutions, meaning that a Georgetown degree received in Qatar will be identical to a Georgetown degree in the U.S..[40]

The level of commitment from the UAE to Education City is high, to helping enable the Emirates to prosper both intellectually and culturally. Large government subsidies provide attractive student financial aid packages on par with those at U.S. Ivy League colleges.[41] Campus administrators from NYU Abu Dhabi are reported to be planning for 40% of the student body to be from the U.S., and their standards will be extraordinarily high: "As we've talked about the admissions process, what we've said is that the students at NYU Abu Dhabi will be students who fit comfortably within the top 1 percent of the talent pool of the world."[42]

By opening foreign campuses or helping to set up universities in countries such as China, India, Singapore and the UAE, U.S. universities is helping to strengthen the our competitors in the race for S&E talent. Wildavsky notes that the U.S. is now facing significantly greater competition for graduating talent. "From China, India and Singapore to Germany, France and Australia, national governments are convinced that competing on the world stage by building great universities will keep more students at home, perhaps attract more from abroad, and above all create innovative and prosperous economies."[43]

"Flood in they do, even though Japan's economy is stagnant and its population is shrinking. Graduates of the standard five-year course at Japan's 57 national colleges of technology, collectively known as Kosen, can each expect about 20 job offers, school officials say. Students who stay on for two years of advanced study receive about 30 offers."[44]

The growth of education in China has been the result of the country's 211 and 985 Projects; government-driven programs for the development of the country's higher education system into a collection of globally competitive research institutions. The 985 Project was created after Chinese President Jiang Zemin declared in 1998 that "universities should play a critical role in implementing the strategy of invigorating the country through science, technology and education," and "China should have several world-class universities of international standard."[45] The central government and local governments have supported 39 universities with almost US$5 billion to date, with more than half of the total invested in the top 9 universities, referred to as the C9 league.[46] The 211 Project, developed in 1995, aims to develop 100 universities at the next level below the 985 Project, and has thus far seen investment at approximately US$2.8 billion.[47]

While the growth of education in India has been difficult, the Wall Street Journal reported in 2012 that India's nearly 200,000 private schools and 17,000 private colleges are seeing significant investment as "the World Bank and private investors are pouring billions of dollars into education there, and the government plans to expand its best-known universities, as well as community colleges. The current five-year plan proposes higher-education investments of more than US$18 billion."[48] At the heart of the matter, however, is the quality of these rapidly-established institutions. The Indian system of education is structured differently than that in the United States and many other Western nations, so many of these institutions are little more than trade schools that provide a narrow set of skills to their graduates for specific positions in the labor market. The globally competent talent that employers require[49] is suggestive of a different type of educational institution, one that bears a stronger resemblance to the top universities of the world.[50]

Developing such high-quality, internationally competitive institutions will require sustained, long-term effort.

Globalization has implications beyond where young engineers are educated; the global nature of the profession and their careers require that they display "global competence," which is characterized by the following:[51]

- Exhibit a global mindset;
- Appreciate and understand different cultures;
- Demonstrate world and local knowledge;
- Effectively communicate cross-culturally, speaking both English and a second language;
- Understand international business, law, and technical elements;
- Live and work in a transnational engineering environment; and
- Work in international teams, both virtual and physical.

Developing an appropriate level of global competence in the next generation of engineers is a serious challenge for educators and employers. According to *Open Doors 2011*, a publication of the International Institute of Education, engineering students accounted for just 3.9% of U.S. students who studied abroad. As Rajala of the IEEE has noted, "to really have an impact, the importance of global competence will have to be valued and given priority."

Courses Unlimited

Current online education efforts are allowing students to access courses without regard to geographic locations or borders. MOOCs, or Massive Open Online Courses, have gained in popularity and have had recent meta-organization via companies like Coursera. A for-profit company started by two computer science professors at Stanford University, Coursera bills itself as "a social entrepreneurship company that partners with the top universities in the world to offer courses online for anyone to take, for free." As of September 2012, 5 months after opening its virtual doors, Coursera had partnered with 33 universities (including a number of Ivy League institutions), and was offering 195 different courses to 1.46 million subscribers. The long-term plan for universities following their aggressive entry into the online course market, however, is not clear. The financial model for MOOCs remains unclear.[52] Coursera co-founder Andrew Ng[53] suggested that Coursera will "probably double its university partnerships at least one more time before it stops recruiting new institutions."

Other companies providing MOOCS include Udacity, an offering of 14 online classes from Stanford University professors with a community of 112,000 students and instructors, and EdX, a collection of seven courses delivered by MIT, Harvard and UC Berkeley instructors, the result of a $60 million investment by MIT and Harvard. Some of the courses include an instructor-signed statement of accomplishment, upon successful completion, for a number of their classes, with some offering students the option of taking a proctored final exam and tests, and even providing job placement assistance.

But will these course offerings be globally successful? The experience of one Indian student illustrates a possible successful future. USA Today reports that Ashwith Rego, 24, of Bangalore, India, recently passed an engineering MOOC taught by an MIT professor, and noted it was more difficult than the work he did in his undergraduate engineering work in India. He stated that "the fact that it was an MIT course, I thought I wouldn't be able to do well … I will definitely put this on my resume."[54] The attachment to highly-regarded universities, programs and instructors may impart a level of global credibility to this alternative form of education.

Inspiration for the current excitement about MOOCs may be attributed to global interest in the Khan Academy, which describes itself as "a not-for-profit with the goal of changing education for the better by providing a free world-class education for anyone anywhere."[55] While the Khan Academy is focused on educating middle and high school students, the group's approach appears to be a model to some degree for the current crop of MOOC providers. In our increasingly connected world, global access to a high-quality, free education from world-recognized and respected universities may even create greater numbers of S&E's on the global stage.

Assessment and evaluation of these alternative educational platforms has yet to be completed. While a given course or platform may boast a large number of student participants, to what extent do the students receive a high-quality learning experience? How does this learning experience fit into students' educational pathways and on-going life-long learning needs of professionals in a rapidly-changing world? Will the existence of MOOCs lead to more narrowly-tailored engineers who have completed specific sets of courses associated with employers technical needs akin to the certifications obtained by IT professionals? Or will these courses further enhance and expand the education of engineers for whom the U.S. college curriculum has become overly crowded? These questions have yet to be addressed and represent an agenda for new engineering educational research.

The Federal Scientist and Engineering Community

Federal agencies employed 235,110 scientists and engineers (S&Es) in 2009, of which 92,867 were engineers.[56] Table 5.3 shows data on Federal employment of S&Es in the most recent year for which detailed agency-level analysis was completed. Of the 86,336 Federally-employed engineers, 58,600 (68%) worked for the Department of Defense (DoD). Within the DoD, 62% of all S&Es are engineers as compared to just 24% of S&Es at all other Federal agencies, reflecting the large role of engineers within the DoD S&E workforce. [57]

	S&Es (2005)	Engineers (2005)	Engineers as a Percent of all S&Es
Department of Defense	93,892	58,600	62%
All other Federal agencies	115,855	27,736	24%
ALL Federal	209,747	86,336	41%

Source: Authors' analysis of data from Proudfoot (2008).

Table 5.3: Federal S&Es, 2005

In most of Federal agencies, and especially in the DoD, the current culture looks skeptically at foreign engagement. Therefore, many Federal managers view international travel and attending conferences in other countries as a highly prized perk or even a boondoggle. Two recent reports suggest that this aversion to international experiences could be undercutting DoD scientists' and engineers' innovative capacity. Independent studies by the Defense Science Board and the National Academies both underscore the importance of international experiences as a means of ensuring that engineers and scientists are globally competent.[58]

Clearly, it is imperative that this mindset be changed but it will likely require mandate from the Executive Branch to initiate the necessary cultural shift. The evidence presented herein indicates this paradigm shift must occur, but two datapoints, in particular, bear this out. First, thirty years ago the U.S. was the world's primary producer of research work, accounting for roughly 70% of the total world production in scientific journals. Today, while the U.S. research community produces roughly the same amount or research work in absolute terms, the U.S. portion of research work conducted across the globe amounts to 30%. Thus, to simply take advantage of the total body of research work done across the world, U.S. Federally-employed scientists and engineers need to be aware of this global body of S&T work to fuel their own innovation engines. Second, view our Federal S&Es for one moment as fully engaged partners in their respective international science and engineering communities. In this capacity they act as a defacto global sensor grid, privy to emerging, potentially disruptive S&E work. This human sensor grid has enormous implications for the U.S. from both economic and national security perspectives. Indeed, this may be the most important function for our national science and engineering community to perform in the coming century.

Agency	2003	2004	2005
All Agencies	206,620	209,994	209,747
Department of Agriculture	19,975	20,550	20,407
Department of Commerce	11,179	11,203	11,293
Department of Defense	92,201	93,972	93,892
Department of the Air Force	16,672	17,192	17,632
Department of the Army	31,310	31,764	31,689
Department of the Navy	37,385	37,842	37,312
Other defense agencies	6,834	7,174	7,259
Department of Energy	4,629	4,545	4,454
Department of Health and Human Services	11,811	11,723	11,542
Department of Housing and Urban Development	324	307	313
Department of the Interior	14,993	15,085	14,933
Department of Justice	2,583	2,653	2,663
Department of Labor	2,445	2,388	2,386
Department of State	1,507	1,751	1,814
Department of Transportation	6,175	6,051	6,011
Department of the Treasury	885	934	938
Department of Veterans Affairs	7,399	7,695	7,061
Environmental Protection Agency	9,838	9,748	9,761
General Services Administration	825	831	841
National Aeronautics and Space Administration	11,029	11,349	11,133
National Science Foundation	496	507	510
Nuclear Regulatory Commission	1,420	1,483	1,534
U.S. International Development Cooperation Agency	191	185	181
All other Agencies	6,715	7,034	7,181

Source: Proudfoot, S. 2008. "Detailed Statistical Tables: Federal Scientists and Engineers: 2003-05" NSF 09-302. (Arlington, VA: National Science Foundation).

Table 5.4: Federal Scientists and Engineers, by Agency: 2003-5

Export Controls

The United States has export control rules that were created during the Cold War, a time when American technology was superior to much of the rest of the world across a broad range of products and knowledge. The rules are in the Export Administration Regulations (EAR) and the International Traffic in Arms Regulations (ITAR). The purpose of export controls is to constrain the use of products and knowledge by those that might choose to use them to do harm. Since the end of the Cold War and with the evolution of a global economy the world has prospered, enabling technological advancement around the globe that rivals American technology. A consequence is that the current system includes what have become with time overly broad descriptions of what is to be controlled. To change some of these rules requires the Congress to first change laws that the EAR and the ITAR are designed to implement.

With the growth in the global economy came truly international corporations, some with research laboratories in multiple countries working on the same problem. Bringing information from their foreign laboratories into their American laboratory is easy, but exporting information from their American laboratory to their foreign laboratories is not as easy, due to current export control rules. When the controls become too cumbersome, a global corporation may choose to exclude participation of their American laboratory. A logical next step is to exclude their American facilities from creating prototypes, and then placing factories near the foreign laboratories. Instead of protecting American technology, the end result of our antiquated export controls is that technology and jobs are lost.

Also irksome are the deemed export rules. A 'deemed export' is the release of an export controlled technology to a foreign national within the borders of the United States. The definition of 'technology' in the law and regulations is difficult to interpret. Deemed exports have proven cumbersome for American universities, particularly those that attract the brightest students from around the world. If a professor has a foreign student in a class, there may be occasions where they can't discuss unclassified educational material in the classroom due to deemed export rules. There may be occasions where the professor will be required to exclude non-citizen students from research, or may not be permitted to publish research findings in academic journals. Such EAR or ITAR violations may be prosecuted in criminal courts.

Early in the first term of the Obama administration, with the encouragement of then Secretary of Defense Robert Gates, the President formed an interagency task force to study export control procedures. Their finding was that the existing export control system is not effectively reducing national security risk. The President accepted the findings, and the U.S. government is now in the process of reforming the export control system with the intent to better protect national security by reducing overly broad descriptions of what is to be controlled.

Conclusion

Globalization of the S&E workforce plays a powerful role in the education and movement of S&E professionals worldwide. While a perceived shortage in the U.S. is debatable, it is clear that the S&E professional of the future will require global competence and will be more migratory, alleviating any current or potential shortage . In spite of international competition, the quality of U.S. engineers and the engineering educational system is still high; indeed, the Massachusetts Institute of Technology continues to top most international lists of top universities. Companies move abroad to expand economic and competitive advantage. Some engineering jobs have been outsourced due to labor cost considerations and R&D operations have been positioned closer to growth markets.[59] Serious deficiencies of engineering graduates from the majority of schools in both India and China are in the process of being ameliorated, but this process will take time. U.S. colleges and universities have moved into the vast educational market represented by both nations to fill this void. Overall, though, the process of globalization is on-going, so it is important that U.S. industry is able to continue to draw the best engineers from the best schools in order to maintain a competitive edge.

As more universities worldwide graduate more S&Es coupled with generous government-supported R&D budgets, an increased volume of scientific information is being created globally and at a more rapid pace than ever before. Clearly in the coming decades, with the frequency of transnational engineering projects increasing significantly as more countries build their own R&D infrastructures and extend their R&D presence to other countries, there will be significant opportunities for innovation in S&T globally. To take advantage of this new age, where a significant knowledge base exists outside its borders, the U.S. has to revisit governmental policies affecting STEM education and S&T R&D budgets in order to insure economic vitality and national security. Reshaping government policies and especially the government culture within its S&T organizations needs to change in order to take advantage of this new, international knowledge base. Doing so will provide additional research fuel for the U.S. innovation engine, which is still the world's leading producer of new ideas. Currently within federal S&T organizations there is a mindset that foreign travel is taboo. This mindset needs to change in order for our federal scientists and engineers to be full participants in the global S&T community. This global S&T engagement will result in both economic and national security benefits of a magnitude which cannot be overstated.

Educational, professional and personal opportunities are all found to be key drivers of globalization. While opportunities abound in developing countries, for now there continues to be a large influx of international students and professionals in S&E fields to the U.S.. However global access to a high-quality, free education from world-recognized and respected universities is likely to change these migration patterns, while creating even greater numbers of S&E's on the global stage. In a shrinking world where mobility is less of a restriction than ever, and where the growing nations are recognizing and addressing shortcomings in their educational systems, the question of whether engineers will become a global commodity appears more a question of 'when' than 'if'. As key innovators, engineers are crucial to technological competitiveness. As such, U.S. industry, universities, professional societies, and government agencies all have a stake in ensuring that the U.S. has a sufficient number of globally competent and highly-skilled engineers that reflect the rich diversity of our nation.

References

1. Wooldridge, A. (2006). The Battle for Brainpower. *The Economist*, 6 October 2006. Retrieved from <http://www.economist.com/node/7961894>
2. Stephens, C. (2009). Engineers Eager to Explore Have Overseas Options. *Houston Chronicle*, November 2009. Retrieved from <http://www.chron.com/jobs/article/Engineers-eager-to-explore-have-overseas-options-1616475.php>
3. Vergano, D. (2010). U.S. Science and Engineering Leadership Facing Foreign Foes. *USA Today*, 25 February 2010. Retrieved from <http://content.usatoday.com/communities/sciencefair/post/2010/02/us-science-and-engineering-leadership-facing-foreign-foes/1#.T-fRgytYs7R>
4. National Science Foundation (2012). *Science and Engineering Indicators 2012*, Arlington, VA (NSB 12-01).
5. Globalization of Science and Engineering Research, A companion to Science and Engineering Indicators 2010. National Science Foundation, Arlington, VA (NSB-10-03), 2010.
6. National Science Foundation (2012). *Science and Engineering Indicators 2012*, National Science Foundation, Arlington, VA (NSB 12-01), Figure 3-45.

7. Ibid. p. 3-56
8. Ibid. p. 4-42
9. Ibid. p. 4-53
10. Ibid. p. 4-53
11. Ibid. p. 4-53
12. Ibid. p. 3-56
13. International Mobility of the Highly Skilled: Policy Brief. *OECD Observer*, 2002.
14. Docquier, F. and Rapoport, H. (2012). Globalization, Brain Drain, and Development. *Journal of Economic Literature*, 50(3): 681–730.
15. Ibid.
16. Department of Homeland Security, U.S. Citizenship and Immigration Services. (2012). Characteristics of H-1B Specialty Occupation Workers, Fiscal Year 2011 Annual Report to Congress, October 1, 2010-September 30, 2011.
17. Bartlett, D.L. (2006). Building A Competitive Workforce: Immigration And The US Manufacturing Sector. *Immigration Daily*, 2006. Retrieved from <http://www.ilw.com/articles/2006,0823-bartlett.shtm>
18. National Science Foundation (2010). *Science and Engineering Indicators 2010*, National Science Foundation, Arlington, VA (NSB 10-01), Chapter 2.
19. SESTAT is comprised of results from three surveys completed by contract organizations for the National Science Foundation: the National Survey of College Graduates; the National Survey of Recent College Graduates; and the Survey of Doctorate Recipients. All are surveys with nationally-representative random samples providing generalizable information about the U.S. science and engineering workforce. For more information see <http://www.nsf.gov/statistics/sestat/>.
20. National Science Foundation (2012). *Science and Engineering Indicators 2012*, National Science Foundation, Arlington, VA (NSB 12-01), p. 3-60.
21. G.M. Turns to the Chinese to Help Sales in India. Global Business with Reuters. *The New York Times*, 5 September 2012. Retrieved from<http://www.nytimes.com/2012/09/06/business/global/gm-turns-to-the-chinese-to-help-sales-in-india.html?_r=0>
22. Howell, V. (2008). *Building a Global Engineering Team*. Institute of Industrial Engineers, 2008 Annual Conference and Expo, Vancouver, BC, Canada, May 17-21, 2008. Retrieved from <http://www.iienet2.org/uploadedfiles/IIE/Technical_Resources/Conference_Proceedings/Annual/96-pres.pdf>

23. Wu, C. (2010). A Sharper Edge. *Prism,* retrieved from <
http://www.prism-magazine.org/mar10/feature_03.cfm
24. National Science Foundation (2012). *Science and Engineering Indicators 2012.* Arlington, VA (NSB 12-01), January 2012, p. 5-37.
25. National Science Foundation (2008). *Science and Engineering Indicators 2008,* Arlington, VA (NSB 08-01), January 2008, Table 5-21.
26. National Science Foundation (2012). *Science and Engineering Indicators 2012,* Arlington, VA (NSB 12-01), January 2012, p. 5-37.
27. McKinsey and Company, (2005). *The Emerging Global Labor Market: Part II – The Supply of Offshore Talent in Services.* Retrieved from <http://www.mckinsey.com/mgi/reports/pdfs/emerginggloballaborm arket/Part2/MGI_supply_executivesummary.pdf>
28. Ibid.
29. Two major periods of expansion for the United States higher education system were the post-Bellum era following the Morrill Land Grant Act of 1863 and the post-World War II era. Both periods were characterized by a rapid proliferation of colleges and universities to meet national needs, especially in engineering. The Land Grant Act was designed to provide higher education to the masses—prior to that time, higher education was largely liberal arts education for the wealthy—with a concurrent expansion of "practical" subjects like science (especially agricultural science) and engineering. After World War II, the GI Bill was used to provide a means of increasing the skills of those who had served during the war and to provide a slower reintegration into the larger economy. The Space Race and Cold War of the post-WWII era combined with the coming of age of baby boomers in the late 1960s and early 1970s led to a second large "growth spurt" for U.S. colleges and universities and another period of expansion for the role of science and engineering in academe.
30. Academic Ranking of World Universities (2011). Retrieved from <http://www.shanghairanking.com/FieldENG2011.html>
31. Kumar, B.V., Finegold, D.L., and Winkler, A-L. (2011). *Will they return? The willingness of potential faculty to return to India and the key factors affecting their decisions.* Tata Institute of Social Sciences, Penn State University, Rutgers School of Management and Labor Relations.
32. Silverstein, M.J. and Singh, A. (2012). Can U.S. Universities Stay on Top?. *The Wall Street Journal,* 28 September 2012.
33. Wildavsky, B. (2010). *The Great Brain Race: How Global Universities Are Reshaping the World,* Princeton University Press.

34. Altbach, P.G. (2011). Is There a Future for U.S. Branch Campuses? *International Higher Education*, Fall 2011, p. 65. Retrieved from <http://www.bc.edu/content/dam/files/research_sites/cihe/pdf/IHEpdfs/ihe65.pdf>

35. Global Higher Education, Branch Campus Listing: 2012. Retrieved from <http://www.globalhighered.org/branchcampuses.php>

36. Grad Schools: Best Engineering Schools, Ranked in 2012. *US News & World Report*, Retrieved from <http://grad-schools.usnews.rankingsandreviews.com/best-graduate-schools/top-engineering-schools/eng-rankings>

37. Lakshman, N. (2009). India to Foreign Colleges: Set Up Campus Here. *Time*. Retrieved from <http://www.time.com/time/world/article/0,8599,1913653,00.html>

38. Chauhan, C. (2012). Dual Degrees with Foreign Universities Get Nod. *Hindustan Times*, New Delhi, 02 June 2012. Retrieved from <http://www.hindustantimes.com/India-news/NewDelhi/Dual-degrees-with-foreign-universities-get-nod/Article1-865060.aspx>

39. Global Higher Education (2012). "C-BERT Interactive Branch Campus Map", accessed October 2012. Retrieved from <http://www.globalhighered.org/maps.php>

40. Wildavsky, B. (2010). *The Great Brain Race: How Global Universities Are Reshaping the World*, Princeton University Press, p. 55.

41. Ibid, p. 45.

42. Ibid, p. 46.

43. Ibid, p. 70.

44. Harden, B. (2011). Japan's Answer to the Skills Gap. *The Washington Post*, 15 October 2011, p. A6.

45. "Building World-Class Universities in China: Shanghai Jiao Tong University". World Bank, p. 35. Retrieved from <http://siteresources.worldbank.org/EDUCATION/Resources/278200-1099079877269/547664-1099079956815/547670-1317659123740/Chapter2.pdf>

46. Ibid.

47. Ibid.

48. Silverstein, M.J. and Singh, A. (2012). Can U.S. Universities Stay on Top?". *The Wall Street Journal*, 28 September 2012.

49. Farrell, D. and Grant. A. (2005). *Addressing China's Looming Talent Shortage*. McKinsey & Company.

50. U.S. News and World Reports (2012). World's Best Universities. Top 400. *U.S. News and World Reports.* Retrieved from <http://www.usnews.com/education/worlds-best-universities-rankings/top-400-universities-in-the-world>; also World University

Rankings 2012/2013. Retrieved from
<http://www.topuniversities.com/university-rankings/world-university-rankings>

51. Warnick, G.M. (2010). *Global Competence: Determination of its Importance for Engineers Working in a Global Environment.* University of Nebraska at Lincoln.

52. Lewin,T. (2012). Education Site Expands Slate of Universities and Courses. *The New York Times*, 19 September 2012. Retrieved from <http://www.nytimes.com/2012/09/19/education/coursera-adds-more-ivy-league-partner-universities.html>

53. Coursera Signs Agreements With Caltech, Duke, EPFL (Lausanne), Georgia Tech, Johns Hopkins, Illinois, Rice, UCSF, University of Edinburgh, University of Toronto, UVA and University of Washington to Offer Classes Online. *The Wall Street Journal*, July 17, 2012.

54. Marklein, M.B. (2012). College May Never Be the Same. *USA Today*, September 12, 2012. Retrieved from <http://www.usatoday.com/news/nation/story/2012/09/12/college-may-never-be-the-same/57752972/1>

55. Khan Academy (2012). Retrieved from <http://www.khanacademy.org>, accessed September 2012.

56. Burrelli, J.S. and Falkenheim, J.C. (2011). *Diversity in the Federal Science and Engineering Workforce.* NSF 11-303. Arlington, VA: National Science Foundation, Division of Science Resource Statistics.

57. Proudfoot, S. (2008). Detailed Statistical Tables: Federal Scientists and Engineers: 2003-05. NSF 09-302. Arlington, VA: National Science Foundation, Science Resource Statistics.

58. National Research Council (2012). "Assuring the U.S. Department of Defense a Strong Science, Technology, Engineering, and Mathematics (STEM) Workforce" Prepublication copy (Washington, DC: National Academies Press). Defense Science Board. "The Report of the Defense Science Board Taskforce on Basic Research" (Washington, DC: Office of the Under Secretary of Defense for Acquisition, Technology and Logistics). Retrieved from: <http://www.acq.osd.mil/dsb/reports/BasicResearch.pdf>

59. Wadhwa, V., Gereffi, G., Rissing, B., and Ong, R. (2007). Where the Engineers Are". *Issues in Science and Technology*, Spring 2007.

Chapter 6

Conclusions and Recommendations

"A nation that depends on innovation for its prosperity, that has unsurpassed universities and research centers, and that has long prided itself on the ingenuity and inventiveness of its technical elite, must devise ways of making solid careers in science once again both captivating and attainable. There's no shortage of American talent. What's in critically short supply are the ideas and determination to use that talent wisely."[1]

Over the past decade, there has been much debate about whether the United States will have the STEM talent, in general, and the engineering talent, in particular, to maintain an innovation edge over other nations. Two nations with large populations in the midst of massive economic transformations—India and China—have been singled out by many analysts as bearing particular scrutiny in the current race to innovate. Both of these nations have undergone significant political transformations that have, within the past decade, led to an economic boom period. Further, both India and China can draw upon a deep pool of expatriate talent, trained internationally but with personal ties back to their homes as an additional engine for science and technology.

Our interest has been primarily centered upon the S&T policy issues affecting the S&T workforce in DOD in general and the U.S. Navy Labs in particular. Six years ago we published in our book *From Science to Seapower-A Roadmap for S&T Revitalization*, ten recommendations. These recommendations were re-visited in a subsequent edition, *Postscript 2010*. The fact remains that the total number of students graduating with a bachelors' degree in engineering in the United States continues to drop as a percentage of the total number of bachelor's degrees awarded. With this in mind we re-examined the issue of workforce revitalization and focused, explicitly, on the engineering community as it is affected by the issues of culture, immigration, demographics and globalization.

The growth of and mass access to U.S. higher education was spurred by the Land Grant Act of 1863 and given an additional boost in the post-World War II era when the GI Bill put college in reach for a generation of Veterans. As the space race and Cold War progressed in the last half of the 20th Century, U.S. higher education institutions came to occupy a position of global supremacy, providing high-quality, research-intensive training for a burgeoning population of international students. Many of these international students have remained in the United States, enriching our culture and economy with their talents. The changing demography of the U.S. population combined with the political and economic changes underway in India and China, have given us pause to consider the extent to which the U.S. will be able to maintain a quality educational system that is foundational to our way of life. In the most recent World Economic Forum Global Innovation Index (GII) publication, for example, the U.S. higher education system's poor track record of retaining entrants to graduation and low production in science and technology were cited to explain the U.S.' continued drop to 10th on innovation rankings.

Our key findings show the following:

There is increasingly intense international competition for skilled S&T workers:

- The United States has dropped to 10th on the Global Innovation Index, a measure of global innovation. While much further down in the rankings overall, China and India were rated as #1 and #2 on global innovation efficiency computed as the ratio of outputs over inputs. Although the U.S. remains the primary destination for international students worldwide, our share of international students decreased from 24% in 2000 to 19% in 2008.[2]
- New educational initiatives such as MOOCs and the Khan Academy, often in partnership with the world's top universities, are offering hundreds of courses to millions of students worldwide. This level of open global access to a high quality free education from world-recognized and respected universities is likely to create greater numbers of S&E's on the global stage.

- Globalization has helped fuel significant growth in high skill migration of technical talent. With digital access to vast resources of information and growing communication networks, engineering has been transformed into a global and 'outsourceable' endeavor. The question of whether engineers will become a global commodity appears more a question of 'how fast' rather than 'if'.
- Nearly half of U.S. adult poll respondents (49%) assumed that the U.S. would remain a technological leader but simultaneously misunderstood the role of engineers in technological advancement.

U.S. engineering has an identity issue and needs to do a better job of attracting diverse students:

- A sizeable portion of the U.S. population remains underrepresented in S&E employment, and more specifically in engineering. Women accounted for just 13% of U.S. engineers in 2009, while African Americans were 5%, and Latinos 6%[3]; yet members of these three groups account for 61% of the U.S. labor force.
- Women of all ethnic groups and men from underrepresented minority groups currently account for 68% of all U.S. college students but represent just 28% of new engineering graduates at the bachelor's level.
- If U.S. women and African American, American Indian and Alaska Native and Latino/Hispanic men earned bachelor's degrees in engineering at the same rate as white men, the U.S. could have produced an additional 67,800 engineering bachelor's-degreed graduates in 2010, nearly doubling the 69,900 U.S. colleges of engineering produced that year.
- The likelihood that U.S. high school students will take a rigorous curriculum that leads to college success varies: while 29% of Asian American students take this curriculum, fewer than 10% of underrepresented minorities and just 14% of white students take this set of classes.
- Unlike U.S students, Indian and Chinese students make their degree field and career choices within a culture that acknowledges the importance of engineering. College-bound Indian and Chinese students spend more time in school, face more competition for college seats, and expend greater effort at academic pursuits than their counterparts in the United States.

Their cultures revere those who succeed in engineering in a way our country's culture does not.

- The implications of the increasing racial and ethnic diversity of the U.S. population for the STEM talent pool is a significant policy issue. Cultural issues associated with African American and Hispanic/Latino communities need to be addressed if we are to be successful in increasing domestic production of U.S. STEM graduates.

Reforming immigration rules would result in an increase in the high-skilled S&E workforce for many years to come.

- Immigration has long provided economic growth and vitality of our economy.[4] Within the past 20 years, though, the immigration visa process has become a major bottleneck in providing additional skilled foreign nationals to supplement our domestic supply of scientists and engineers.
- 61% of Asian immigrant adults (aged 25 to 64) have at least a bachelor's degree, twice the rate of non-Asian immigrants making recent Asian arrivals the most highly educated cohort of immigrants in U.S. history.[5]
- Both immigrants and their children were found to 'hit above their weight' in S&E at high school competitions and in entrepreneurial ventures, founding companies in the U.S. that both employ millions of people and generate trillions of dollars in revenue.

Large countries like China and India are dedicating resources to developing infrastructure, including educational institutions, transportation and energy systems. In addition, the investment by large multinational corporations in these same nations has drawn international analysts' attention to their science and technology potential. As we discussed earlier, the status accorded engineering in these nations is far greater than that in the United States. Even though the economies of these nations may have difficulties employing all of the engineers its institutions produce, this is likely to be a market-clearing mechanism. As the market clears and the institutions with the quality graduates are able to persist and to further intensify research activity by recruiting the best researchers, the long-term innovative potential of such large economies is vast.

The Path Forward: Revitalizing U.S. Engineering

How best can the United States ensure the vitality of our engineering workforce? First, it is important to understand what U.S. engineers will need to be globally competitive. There is no dearth of prescriptive advice about the skills the 21st Century workforce needs. Without question, engineers need a foundation of technical skill in core subjects but that core must have space for topics that have often been eschewed. The humanities and social sciences are likely to provide the critical thinking, adaptability, and multicultural skillset that engineers will need to be able to communicate and work effectively with teams of diverse, often geographically-distant colleagues.

Also, foreign language proficiency is an increasingly necessary skill in the flatter world, as it engenders a deeper understanding of the cultural dimension of the global technical community. Engineering programs do not often have foreign language requirements, which have also become far less prevalent among graduate programs. There are occasional programs that stand apart. The University of Rhode Island engineering school has a five-year dual degree program in which students earn a B.S. in an engineering field and a B.A. in a foreign language. As part of the program, students complete an internship at a company in a country where they can practice their chosen language. This is an innovative program that appeals, especially to women who generally account for a third of the students in the dual program.

While continuing education has long been a critical aspect of engineers' professional life, the pace of technological change and the competitive pressures of a global labor market indicate that life-long learning will be even more important to engineers. In the past, engineers were encouraged to pursue graduate work in their own or other engineering disciplines (e.g., systems engineering) or to pursue an MBA via traditional graduate study. Many companies have their own continuing education programs, as well, meant to provide engineers with more focused training. The implications of Massive Open Online Courses (MOOCs) for on-going engineers' education remain to be seen. The National Science Foundation and the U.S. Department of Education, two of the primary funders of U.S. educational research, should ensure that the implications of MOOCs are documented and disseminated with insights about the efficacy of MOOCs to provide quality training/re-training to engineers and other workers.

Culture and Messaging

The highly decentralized U.S. education system poses special barriers for meeting national-level challenges. The responsibility for curriculum change resides at state and local levels. For example, a number of educational initiatives that have been proposed to revitalize U.S. pre-college STEM education require state policy action. These include ideas such as:

- Introducing engineering for all K through 12 students
- Parental involvement in STEM education
- Changes to the structure of the school year (e.g. longer days, year-round schooling, etc.)
- The implementation of blended instruction, taking better advantage of technology
- Greater compensation for skilled science/math/engineering teachers
- Getting back to fundamentals in math education
- Calculator free schools through certain grades
- Magnet and charter schools

To different degrees, many of these ideas have received attention from educational researchers. National-level resources such as the "what works clearinghouse" maintained by the Department of Education, provide a mechanism by which such research findings can be accessed by local authorities. In addition, in the past ten years, the U.S. Department of Education has implemented a new funding stream, the Investing in Innovation or I3 awards,[6] which are meant to encourage local educational authorities to test out innovative approaches to education and to subject these innovations to rigorous evaluation to determine the efficacy of the innovations as well as the ways in which those that are successful may be scaled up or more widely implemented. New awardees in the 2012 funding cycle are required to secure a private partner contribution, so that these projects will demonstrate how public-private partnerships might be useful in addressing the nation's educational challenges.

Many observers have suggested that pre-college teachers in STEM fields need to be compensated at a higher rate than their non-STEM counterparts because of concerns about STEM teachers leaving teaching. The Business Higher Education Forum in collaboration with Raytheon has developed a system dynamics model of the U.S. pre-college education system, which shows that such a two-tiered compensation scheme would not actually solve the problem of teacher attrition because the industries that lure teachers away would merely increase the financial incentives to overcome the differential.[7] The research to date on teacher attrition indicates that mathematics and science teachers are as likely as teachers in other subjects to leave the field, suggesting that increasing compensation may not result in higher retention. Teachers who leave cite lack of classroom autonomy, student discipline problems and the extent to which they received useful, content-specific professional development among the top reasons for leaving.[8]

Engineering professional societies and collaborations between other STEM professional societies like the National Science Teachers' Association, need to continue current efforts and to intensify implementation of the recommendations in the National Academies' study on "Changing the Conversation" about engineering. As we have discussed, engineers contribute greatly to solving some of the world's biggest societal problems, but better messaging about the field is necessary to educate a wider public and more diverse students about engineers' powerful toolkit. According to the 2009 High School Transcript Study by the U.S. Department of Education, 3% of U.S. high school graduates in 2009 had taken an engineering class while they were in high school. While this is a change over the 0% that had done so in 1990, very few U.S. students have early exposure to engineering. While it remains for states to implement new curriculum policy, professional societies can work to provide support to states to bring about these changes.

Engineering professional societies can also play an important role in elevating the profile of engineering and of showing how engineering can solve global humanitarian challenges. For example, attention could be directed to the work of groups like Engineers Without Borders, a group that works to solve such humanitarian problems as providing fresh water and developing clean and inexpensive energy.

Increasing the Participation of Underrepresented Groups

Better messaging about engineering, described previously, could increase the allure of engineering for young women from all groups. But to address the previously discussed issues that negatively impact the ability of African Americans, American Indians and Alaska Natives and Latinos/Hispanics (both women and men) to successfully complete engineering programs requires additional effort, largely at the state and local levels. Because two-year colleges are the initial starting point for many minority students, state governments should implement effective articulation agreements between two-year and four-year institutions.

While articulation agreements are no longer new, monitoring these agreements and ensuring that they provide effective pathways into four-year programs represent additional hard work left to do. In particular, the course content and not merely the title of the course, needs to be in alignment in order for students to truly reap the benefits associated with attending a two-year school.[9] In addition, anecdotal evidence suggests that dual enrollment programs, in which students are simultaneously enrolled in a two-year and a four-year institution, provide students with a stronger attachment to the four-year institution so that they are more likely to successfully transition from the two-year to the four-year school.

While there are individual benefits associated with students' completion of the first two years of college at a community college, it is important to document the societal benefits as well. Community colleges are often far less costly than four-year institutions, which enables students to save money on tuition and also on room and board costs if they are able to live at home. At a societal level, the lower costs mean that there are fewer dollars needed for Pell Grants and guaranteed student loans. Furthermore, community colleges' focus on undergraduate education versus the multifaceted foci of four-year colleges and universities further suggests some efficiencies associated with implementing a stronger emphasis on students starting at the two-year rather than four-year level.

Secondary schools in high-poverty areas, which also tend to have high enrollments of African American, American Indian and Latino/Hispanic children, are also more likely to face greater challenges in employing high quality teachers in core subjects. According to analysis by the Education Trust, in low-poverty schools 11% of high school mathematics classes were taught by teachers either without a certification or college major in mathematics, in high-poverty schools 25% of mathematics classes were taught by out-of-field teachers.[10] According to the most recent Schools and Staffing Survey (SASS) data, 95.5% of high school teachers who taught science classes were either certified to teach in science or had earned a college degree in science, but at those schools where more than half students were African American, just 87% of science teachers were either certified to teach or degreed in science.[11]

States need to develop and implement robust systems of assessment and evaluation of teacher quality to ensure that all students, regardless of ethnicity or economic background, have access to high quality teachers who have requisite skills to teach the subjects they have been assigned.[12] Implementation of such systems is more imperative schools with higher enrollments of ethnic minority students and those from economically disadvantaged backgrounds.

Dealing with a Flatter World

In addition to the skills, discussed earlier, that engineers need to be globally competitive, there are issues associated with systemic aspects of the challenges presented by globalization. National progress in addressing the concerns laid out in the *Rising Above the Gathering Storm* reports needs to be embraced, ideally by an organization like the National Center for Science and Engineering Statistics (NCSES, formerly the Division of Science Resource Statistics at the National Science Foundation) in cooperation with the National Center for Education Statistics (NCES). The biennial "Science and Engineering Indicators" report would be the ideal way to provide the nation with a scorecard on implementation of the *Rising Above the Gathering Storm* recommended action plan.

Globalization of the STEM workforce, in general, and the engineering workforce, in particular, must be addressed in a meaningful way to ensure that U.S. firms are able to make the most efficient use of high-quality talent. For example, rewriting ITAR and EAR export controls needs to be done to reflect the new world order. The unintended consequences of the current—antiquated—export controls need to be determined and a new set established so that U.S. firms are not hamstrung in international research, development and innovation processes.

At the national level, we need to actively pursue a strategy of engagement with other countries. A key element of this engagement would actively involve students, at all levels, in this enterprise. Examples include the following:

- K-12 students should be required to demonstrate a working knowledge of international affairs, and be able to speak at least one other language.
- Formal partnerships should be established between elementary, middle and high schools with similar education levels in other countries.
- The Department of Education should lead an effort to connect a significant number of our schools with those of other countries and to be fully engaged across the globe within a decade. This could include establishing a more robust formal teacher exchange program with other countries.

Within the Federal sector, a true cultural shift needs to occur. Currently foreign travel is often viewed as a boondoggle and, therefore, difficult in general, but nearly impossible for S&Es employed by the Department of Defense. Anecdotal evidence shows many instances where technical staff has simply not attempted to request attending an international conference due to the layers of approval that must be obtained. This mindset must change in order for our scientists and engineers to engage their peers across the globe.

There are two primary reasons to access the emerging body of research work being done in other countries. The first is to provide additional research fuel to the U.S. innovation engine. Thirty years ago the U.S. produced roughly 70% of the research work across the globe. Today the U.S. percentage of total world production of research is near 30%, although interestingly enough, the absolute production level of research in the U.S. has remained constant. Thus, simply from a return on investment viewpoint there is research work being done in other countries which we can use in our innovation system within the U.S. that simply makes economic sense.

The second reason for our scientists and engineers to engage in a more robust fashion with their international technical peers is the resultant global S&T awareness network capable of providing early warning of potentially disruptive technologies, either from an economic or defense perspective. Our entire cadre of Federal scientists and engineers working at the frontiers of technology should have a mandate that would include attending at least one international conference outside the U.S. every two years, and submitting a thorough trip report so as to inform others in the U.S. on international developments across the globe. It is imperative that our federal technical establishment be a full and equal player in the global S&T community.

Finally, U.S. immigration policy is in need, once again, of careful yet comprehensive reform. Over the past four years, efforts at reform have been stalled by a deeply-divided Congress. Meanwhile, entrepreneurs who may have initially considered coming to or staying in the United States have shifted operations to countries that have similarly well-trained labor forces but within a less cumbersome regulatory environment.[13]

Our recommendations include:

1.   Monitor progress of the American COMPETES Act.

- The NSF's National Center for Science and Engineering Statistics (NCSES, formerly Science Resource Statistics) should be charged with monitoring the indicator data associated with COMPETES and the *Rising Above the Gathering Storm* report.

- The National Science Board in collaboration with the Defense Science Board and the President's Council of Advisors on Science and Technology (PCAST) should be tasked with reviewing data on regular basis and reporting their findings to Congress.

The National Academies have convened occasional committees in its Board on Science Education. A recent committee, for example, has completed a report titled "Monitoring Progress Toward Successful K-12 STEM Education: A Nation Advancing?". The National Science and Technology Council Committee on STEM Education (also known as CoSTEM) was formed in 2010 to coordinate Federal programs and activities in support of STEM education (Sec. 101 of the America COMPETES Reauthorization Act). While these are important activities, providing a research base and enabling cooperation across the Federal government for STEM education, the plan of action described in *Rising Above the Gathering Storm* will need more focused attention by a body with both the expertise to measure progress and the authority to act, as necessary. As suggested earlier, the NCSES should be charged with monitoring the indicator data associated with COMPETES and the *Rising Above the Gathering Storm* report. The National Science Board in collaboration with the Defense Science Board and the President's Council of Advisors on Science and Technology (PCAST) should all be tasked with reviewing these data on regular basis and reporting their findings to Congress.

2.   Expand the role of the National Science Foundation in K-12 STEM education.

The National Science Foundation should play a stronger role in K-12 STEM education. NSF in collaboration with DOED should create a pilot national STEM education center – akin to the engineering research centers. The Center could:

- Establish K-12 STEM teacher training and certification;
- Provide on-going professional development for STEM teachers;[14] and
- Promote and disseminate high-quality pedagogical research on STEM education.

The Department of Defense could take a leadership role in developing this center in affiliation with one of its educational institutions, such as the Naval Postgraduate School, as a pilot program that could later be expanded to more regional centers throughout the country. These regional centers would have a focused, state of the art research-driven curriculum to raise the bar in the U.S. for STEM teacher quality.

3.   **Encourage professional engineering societies to take a lead role in engineering messaging and engagement at the high school level and enhancing diversity in the profession. Professional societies should:**

- Encourage engineering as a profession of choice for young students through improved messaging.
- Establish high school chapters similar to those at colleges and universities to provide meaningful connections between high school students, college engineering students and professional engineers.
- Ensure that organizational strategic plans and national platforms explicitly embrace diversity.

The National Academy of Engineering report, *Changing the Conversation*, provides a useful toolkit for engineers to more effectively conduct outreach to capture the imagination of potential new students, especially those who have been traditionally underrepresented in engineering. Further, professional engineering societies should ensure that organizational strategic plans and national platforms explicitly embrace diversity.

4.   **Encourage efforts to develop virtual academies for STEM subjects, such as the Khan Academy.**

The National Science Foundation, Department of Education, ONR, and others should encourage virtual STEM academy content development as a cooperative activity with our international partners. It is envisioned that as a result of these efforts, there would be a plethora of academies covering all subjects, with comprehensive STEM components. A nationally available virtual resource should also be developed as an ongoing self-training program for science, math and engineering educators. The program, co-developed with the aforementioned K-12 STEM pilot center, would give STEM educators an opportunity to be knowledgeable of emerging trends and particular areas of interest in science and engineering, and help further elevate the capabilities of the entire body of science and math teachers. These entities should take a lead in developing assessment and "consumer guides" for these programs.

5.   Streamline the visa process for foreign S&T students and professionals.

Improvement of the current visa process through the U.S. Citizenship and Immigration Services (USCIS) is a key focus, but would constitute only part of significant and overdue immigration reform. A revision of immigration policy should be co-developed between major S&E employers and relevant government organizations. There should be careful evaluation of and emphasis on high-demand STEM skills for visa applicants, with a streamlined process to increase efficiency and reduce wait-times. In a similar vein, as is the case with Australia's SkillSelect program, allowances for immigrant numbers in key fields of need could be on a sliding scale, as determined by annual market demand projections from the Bureau of Labor Statistics. There also needs to be a clear pathway to citizenship for S&Es who desire it, both for those coming into the country and those who have completed degrees at our educational institutions, to avoid the 'reverse brain drain' phenomenon.

6.   Actively develop underrepresented group representation in pathways to engineering careers.

Engineering colleges should create a senior administrative position to attend to the need to increase the presence of groups traditionally underrepresented in engineering. Many universities have established such offices previously, with mixed results, generally associated with a lack of sufficient budget, staff and power to effect necessary actions within the college of engineering to increase student diversity. In some cases, colleges have split a small set of resources between a Women in Engineering program and a Minority Engineering program (or variants of these) only to find that neither program was effectively resourced. Such programs need to move beyond being "feel good" efforts and require the kind of influence necessary to implement changes that will achieve meaningful goals and objectives. Strategies successfully used in other fields should also be explored to increase the number of engineers from groups underrepresented in engineering. As an example, since 1972, the National Health Service Corps program has provided both medical program scholarships and loan repayments in return for meeting service requirements in underserved communities. In a similar manner, the

National Defense Education Program's Science, Mathematics, and Research for Transformation (SMART) program could use scholarships-for-service to increase participation in engineering by groups underrepresented in the field for the DoD.

7.   **Require states to pursue a stronger role for community colleges.**

- States should monitor and increase the efficacy of articulation agreements to provide students with a true pathway from the two-year to four-year degree.
- States should mediate program development so that two year STEM programs are co-developed with four year institutions to allow an easier transition between the two institutions.
- Dual enrollment programs should be developed so that students form an early connection to both the two-year and the four-year institution.
- Implement state-level articulation agreements rather than ones that are forged between two institutions independent of state regulatory authorities.

Individual states should encourage a stronger role for community colleges as these are the key entry institutions for an increasing number of diverse students. Many Latino/Hispanic youth initiate their college studies at less-expensive two-year colleges close to home, former members of the armed services often reintegrate into higher education via these institutions, and many workers retrain for new skills in our rapidly-changing economy at nimble two-year institutions. Articulation agreements have become commonplace: these are a step in the right direction. But state-level agreements, stronger formal connections between two-year and four-year institutions, and dual enrollment programs all are necessary institutional innovations that increase the efficacy of these articulation agreements to provide students with a true pathway from the two-year to four-year degree.

8.   **Benchmark U.S. STEM education against high performing OECD countries, and provide funding for rigorous evaluation of STEM education.**

U.S. STEM education performance should be benchmarked against high performing OECD countries. Education expenditure adjustments should be made as appropriate to the end goal of performing at or exceeding the levels in these countries. As a key component of this effort, a comprehensive examination of current STEM expenditures should be undertaken. Efforts are already underway to increase accountability for public funds expenditures, among which are included education expenditures. New guidance from the Office of Management and Budget, for example, indicates that Federal agencies should be using evidence and evaluation to improve programmatic performance and as a basis for making decisions about programs on an on-going basis. Recent guidance from the General Accountability Office as well as the competitive i3 grants that have been funded by the DOED in the past couple of years underscore the role of high-quality, rigorous evaluation as a means to improve education. STEM education should be subjected to careful assessment and evaluation, with sufficient funding provided for independent assessments and evaluations.

9.   The President should issue an Executive Order that encourages engagement of Federal scientists and engineers in the global S&T community.

The challenges of globalization run head-long into Federal work rules and practices that make it nearly impossible for Federally-employed S&Es to keep up with their fields. Yet international experiences are becoming even more prevalent in other sectors (i.e., academia and private-sector employers). Our entire cadre of federal scientists and engineers working at the frontiers of technology should attend at least one international conference outside the U.S. every two years, with a further requirement to inform others on international R&D efforts. As a result of these actions we will have a global S&T awareness network capable of providing early warning of potentially disruptive technologies, either from an economic or defense perspective. It is imperative that our federal technical establishment be a full and equal player in the global S&T community.

In conclusion, the authors assert the vitality of the engineering workforce is a national issue, from both an economic and national security perspective. This issue is also complex, requiring serious thought, and does not lend itself to easy, simple solutions. The U.S. position of dominance in S&T is being reshaped by a number of key factors. Globalization has flattened the world, speeding communications and the rapid exchange of ideas, creating diffusion of innovation and providing greater access to a deepening global engineering labor pool. The U.S. system of education remains decentralized, with large disparities in state and local standards and a persistent lack of equitable opportunities for all.

Engineering, as a profession, suffers from an image problem in this country: most Americans have little understanding of the key role engineers play in meeting technological challenges, nor of the innovative work that engineers do that addresses humanitarian issues. Many of the most talented members of our current engineering workforce are immigrants, yet we struggle to reform our immigration policy to allow more into the country. We also do not appropriately tap into the pool of talent in underrepresented groups, in order to further add to the diversity of thought, a key component of the U.S. innovation engine. At the present time we continue to enjoy dominance in the area of national defense, yet this position is threatened by the same forces that have led our nation to drop to tenth place, globally, in innovation. Unless we are able to tap a larger pool of STEM talent—including those who are already U.S. citizens as well as those who bring their talents to our nation—our security will become increasingly tenuous while other nations-such as China and India, as discussed here—move into more superior positions. Threats to our defense will continue to multiply and diversify in coming years: our nation needs a revitalized S&T workforce to effectively meet current and future challenges and preserve our way of life.

References

1. Benderly, B.L. (2010). The Real Science Gap. *Pacific Standard,* 14 June 2010. Retrieved from <http://www.psmag.com/science/the-real-science-gap-16191/>
2. National Science Foundation (2012). *Science and Engineering Indicators, 2012*, Chapter 2, p. 2-5.
3. Frehill, L.M. (2010). *Fact Sheet: U.S. Engineering Work Force* White Plains, NY: NACME, Inc. Note: "All engineering occupations" includes "engineering managers," "engineers," "engineering technicians," and "sales engineers."
4. Lieberson, S. (1981). *A Piece of the Pie: Blacks and White Immigrants Since 1880.* Berkeley, CA: University of California Press.
5. Pew Research Center (2012). "The Rise of Asian Americans", Social and Demographic Trends, June 2012, p. 1.
6. U.S. Department of Education. (2012). Retrieved from <http://www2.ed.gov/programs/innovation/index.html>
7. Business-Higher Education Forum (2011). *U.S. STEM Education Model.* Retrieved from <http://forio.com/simulate/bhef/u-s-stem-education-model/overview/>

8. Ingersoll, R.M. and May, H. (2010). *The Magnitude, Destinations, and Determinants of Mathematics and Science Teacher Turnover*, Philadelphia, PA: Consortium for Policy Research in Education. Retrieved from <http://www.gse.upenn.edu/pdf/rmi/MathSciTeacherTurnover.pdf>, accessed November 11, 2012.

9. Tilsley, A. (1 November 2012). *STEM Pathways*. Inside Higher Education. Retrieved from <http://www.insidehighered.com/news/2012/11/01/new-focus-helping-community-college-students-stem-fields-four-year-degree>. See also Packard, B., Gagnon, J.L., LaBelle, O., Jeffers, K., and Lynn, E. (2011). "Women's Experiences in The Stem Community College Transfer Pathway*" Journal of Women and Minorities in Science and Engineering* 17(2), 129–147.

10. Almy, S. and Theokas, C. (November 2010). *Not Prepared for Class: High-Poverty Schools Continue to Have Fewer In-Field Teachers.* Washington, DC: The Education Trust. Retrieved from <http://www.edtrust.org/sites/edtrust.org/files/publications/files/Not%20Prepared%20for%20Class.pdf>

11. U.S. Department of Education, National Center for Education Statistics (2010). *Status and Trends in the Education of Racial and Ethnic Minorities*, NCES 2010-015, Table 9.1.

12. There are efforts underway to measure teacher quality. The Teacher Performance Assessment Consortium (http://aacte.org/index.php?/Programs/Teacher-Performance-Assessment-Consortium-TPAC/teacher-performance-assessment-consortium.html) and a project that focuses on mathematics education, (http://www.gse.harvard.edu/ncte/projects/project1/default.php) are two examples in addition to the work underway at The Education Trust (www.edtrust.org).

13. Report by the Partnership for a New American Economy (August 2012). *Open for Business: How Immigrants are Driving Small Business Creation in the United States.* Retrieved from <http://www.renewoureconomy.org/sites/all/themes/pnae/openforbusiness.pdf>
See also: Wadhwa, V. (2002). *The Immigrant Exodus: Why America Is Losing the Global Race to Capture Entrepreneurial Talent.* Wharton Digital Press. Retrieved from <http://wdp.wharton.upenn.edu/books/the-immigrant-exodus/>

14. National Research Council (2012). *Monitoring Progress Toward Successful K-12 STEM Education: A Nation Advancing?* prepublication copy. Washington, DC; National Academies Press.

Appendix

The Community Speaks

"Why is it socially acceptable to say that you're bad at math but not socially acceptable to say you're bad at reading?"[1]

[Remarks by Barack Obama]
    The key to our success—as it has always been—will be to compete by developing new products, by generating new industries, by maintaining our role as the world's engine of scientific discovery and technological innovation. It's absolutely essential to our future.[2]

    The problem is that American engineering institutions and policies focus primarily on the traditional 18- to 24-year-old student, while, as noted by Tony Carnevale of Georgetown University, "Lifelong learning has become an applause line in everybody's stump speech but has yet to become a line item of any consequence in public budgets."

    Changing the postdegree learning culture among engineers in the United States is a tall order. But it's doable, and it's a lot easier than playing catch-up if the rest of the world passes us by. As Daniel Laughlin of NASA put it, we should be "preparing students for jobs that don't yet exist, using technologies that haven't been invented, in order to solve problems we don't even know are problems yet."[3]

Recommendations from Successful K-12 STEM Education (2011)	Indicators
Districts Should Consider Multiple Models of STEM-Focused Schools	1. Number of, and enrollment in, STEM-focused schools and programs in each district.
Districts Should Devote Adequate Instructional Time and Resources to Science in Grade K-5	2. **Time allocated to teach science in K-5.** 3. Science-related learning opportunities in elementary schools.
Districts Should Ensure that their Science and Mathematics Curricula are Focused on the Most Important Topics in Each Discipline, are Rigorous, and are Articulated as a Sequence of Topics and Performances	4. **Adoption of instructional materials in grades K-12 that embody Common Core State Standards in Mathematics and A framework for K-12 Science Education.** 5. **Classroom coverage of content and practices in Common Core and A Framework for K-12 Science Education.**
Districts Need to Enhance the Capacity of K-12 Teachers	6. **Teachers' science and mathematics content knowledge for teaching.** 7. Teachers' participation in STEM-specific professional development activities.
Districts Should Provide Instructional Leaders with Professional Development that Helps them to Create the School Conditions that Appear to Support Student Achievement	8. Instructional leaders' participation in professional development on creating conditions that support STEM learning.
Policy Makers at the National, State, and Local Levels Should Elevate Science to the Same Level of Importance as Reading and Mathematics	9. **Inclusion of science in federal and state accountability systems.** 10. Proportion of major federal K-12 education initiatives that include science. 11. State and district staff dedicated to supporting science instruction.
States and National Organizations Should Develop Effective Systems of Assessment that are Aligned with a Framework for K-12 Science Education and that Emphasize Science Practices Rather Than Mere Factual Recall	12. States' use of assessments that measure the core concepts and practices of science and mathematics disciplines.
National and State Policy Makers Should Invest in a Coherent, Focused, and Sustained Set of Supports for Stem Teachers	13. State and federal expenditures dedicated to improving the K-12 STEM teaching workforce.
Federal Agencies Should Support Research that Disentangles the Effect of School Practice from Student Selection, Recognizes the Importance of Contextual Variables, and Allows for Longitudinal Assessment of Student Outcomes	14. **Federal funding for the three broad kinds of research identified in Successful K-12 STEM Education.**

Table A.1: Committee on an Evaluation Framework for Successful K-12 STEM Education

Following a 2011 report by the National Research Council (NRC) on successful K-12 education in science, technology, engineering, and mathematics (STEM), Congress asked the National Science Foundation to identify methods for tracking progress toward the report's recommendations. In response, the NRC convened the Committee on an Evaluation Framework for Successful K-12 STEM Education to take on this assignment.

The committee developed 14 indicators linked to the 2011 report's recommendations, shown in Table A1. By providing a focused set of key indicators related to students' access to quality learning, educators' capacity, and policy and funding initiatives in STEM, the committee addresses the need for research and data that can be used to monitor progress in K-12 STEM education and make informed decisions about improving it. All 14 indicators are intended to form the core of this system. However, the indicators highlighted in bold in the table—2, 4, 5, 6, 9, and 14—reflect the committee's highest priorities.[4]

What does it mean to be college-ready? Half the states in the country have agreed on a definition. And that definition will shape the way student performance is judged in those states in a couple years.

The Partnership for Assessment of Readiness for College and Careers, or PARCC, has approved a set of descriptors for the tests it's designing for the Common Core State Standards. They lay out how many levels of achievement there will be on the test, specify what level a student has to reach to be considered "college ready," and describe the level of expertise students must show to merit that title.

PARCC's policy will be that students earn the "college readiness" determination by performing at level 4 on a 5-level test. Reaching that level on the language arts part of the exam will mean that students have "demonstrated the academic knowledge, skills, and practices necessary" to skip remedial classes and go directly into entry-level, credit-bearing courses in "college English composition, literature, and technical courses requiring college-level reading and writing." Scoring at level 4 in math allows students to enroll directly in entry-level, credit-bearing courses in algebra, introductory statistics, and "technical courses requiring an equivalent level" of math.

The PARCC policy says that college-readiness scores on the test will be set in such a way that students who score at that level-level 4-will have a 75 percent chance of earning a grade of C or better in those college courses.

Acknowledging a sensitive area in the discussion of college readiness, the policy notes that the skills sought in the tests are only the "academic" ones necessary for college success, not the entire spectrum of skills necessary, such as persistence or motivation. It also makes sure to note that the tests aren't being designed for admissions purposes, or to place students in more advanced college courses.[5]

[Remarks of Richard D. Stephens, Senior Vice President for Human Resources and Administration, The Boeing Company]

There are engineering schools today that are achieving graduation rates that are upwards of 80%, from entering freshmen to 4 or 5 or 6 years later, engineers come out the other end. I think that's the model, and there are four things they tend to do.

One: What do we all want when we go start something new? We want a role model, we want a mentor, we want something to help us out, so the truly effective engineering schools are getting the right yields, they assign students to a cohort of fifty students. So they get the help and the monitoring in those first few years.

Two: The highest dropout rates in engineering school tend to be physics and mathematics. The schools that are very successful somehow get real practical applications into what's going on, so they not only learn the concepts, but they learn how to apply it.

Three: When many of us were going to school we weren't allowed to be involved in projects because we didn't know enough. The schools that are successful get their kids involved from day one in freshman projects because they say "now, I can go solve problems".

Four: I believe the Academy ought to hold business accountable for this is, for successful engineering schools to get the right yield, is to make sure their students have internships between at least their sophomore and junior year. And you ought to demand more of us in engineering to help create those, because we're the ones that want the real hands-on, practical experience.[6]

[Remarks of Dr. Linda P. Katehi, Chancellor of University of California, Davis]

As engineers ... very little have we cared about the social impact of what we create. We identify a problem, and we try to identify the best possible solution. But I think in a flat world where our technology tools become widely available, it is very important for us to become socially aware, and socially responsible for the solutions we provide. And I think we need to start with that thinking very early. I also believe that social sciences for the 21st century will play a fundamental role in engineering, and we need to think that way as we develop our curricula, and as we teach math and science to kids.[7]

For a society that is leading technologically, and a society that has a citizenry that needs to make informed decisions about technologies, it's not just that we do not produce engineers, it's that we do not produce citizens who are technologically literate, or science literate, and that is a big question we have to address.[8]

The science and economics of large-scale increases in support of science and technology are clear. As usual, the politics is the problem.[9]

[Remarks by Michelle Obama at NSF]

I know for me, I'm a lawyer because I was bad at these subjects. (Laughter) All lawyers in the room, you know it's true. We can't add and subtract, so we argue. (Laughter).[10]

Rockwell, ASME's president, stated in an interview with Chron.com that when she started her career, she felt that women were "actively discouraged" from entering professions related to science and engineering. Rockwell persevered and pursued a career in engineering. The profession of engineering employed so few women, that when she first walked onto a construction site early in her career, all of the workers stopped and stared.[11]

Ever since the first elementary school teacher rolled the first television set into the first classroom to air the first course offering from "educational television," there's been the hope and the promise that technology would revolutionize the way teaching and learning would be done.

As things turned out, educational television became public television and went off in a different direction. And despite the advent of the personal computer and the Internet, most education today remains much like it's been for hundreds of years: one teacher, 30 kids, textbooks and a blackboard.

Now that's about to change. The cost of education has gotten so high, student achievement has become so disappointing, and the technology and computerized pedagogy are now sufficiently developed and ubiquitous that the long-awaited revolution in education is about to begin.[12]

[Remarks of Dr. Anant Argwal, President, edX and Professor, MIT]

In our first course we offered in Spring of this year, with zero marketing dollars, we [edX] had 155,000 students worldwide take the course. And, truth in advertising, we advertised it as a hard course, in fact, we advertised it as an MIT-hard course, and we said second order differential equations and complex analysis are pre-requisites to keep people away. And 155,000 students signed up for the course, 7,200 students passed this really hard course, and that's as many students as would take the class at MIT in 40 years. ... We taught that class with about the same level of staffing as we would teach a one semester course at MIT, which about 100-200 students take.[13]

A report by the National Center on Time & Learning cites studies suggesting that science instruction in the elementary grades has increasingly been squeezed out of the curriculum. The report, "Strengthening Science Education: The Power of More Time to Deepen Inquiry and Engagement," makes the case for devoting more learning time for science and looks at case studies of promising approaches to make the most of that extra time.[14]

Still, as many as 60 percent of students who enter college with the intention of majoring in science and math change their plans. Because so many students intend to major in a STEM subject but don't follow through, many observers have assumed that universities are where the trouble starts. I beg to differ.

Perhaps more than English or history, STEM subjects require an enormous amount of foundational learning before students can become competent. Students usually reach graduate school before they can hope to make an original contribution. They can experiment in high school labs, but the U.S. schools' approach to math and science lacks, in large part, a creative element. We need to help students understand that math and science are cumulative disciplines, and help them enjoy learning even as they gradually build a base of knowledge.

Without firsthand experience of the scientific method and its eventual pay-off, students will continue to flock to other majors when their science and math courses become too demanding. If we want more scientists and engineers later, we need to teach children about the joys of hard work and discovery now.[15]

Our job market has accommodated over 40 million more women in the workforce since 1960. The number of full-time, year-round women in the workforce has grown more than 350 percent, to 42.8 million workers, according to 2010 Census data.

If there is an income divide in America it is over education, and this makes sense: People who are better educated should make more money.

Politically incorrect as it sounds, poverty is driven by a lack of education and by single- parent households. Married couples have a median income of $72,751. Female-headed households with no husband have a median income of $32,031. Some will say that the number of female-only households living in poverty has doubled since 1965, to more than 15 million.[16]

For nearly 20 years, high school chemistry teacher Jonathan Bergmann would teach a lesson in class, help students after school and give them standard homework assignments. He was good enough to win a teacher award. But seven years ago, he and Aaron Sams, another teacher at Woodland Park High School in Colorado, decided to do something different.

The initial impetus was reducing the time kids spend with teachers after school. The result has been a total rethinking of how classrooms operate, all based on a question every teacher should be asking: "What is the best use of our face-to-face class time?" The answer for Bergmann: turning his class upside down.

What exactly is a flipped classroom? In the simplest form, basically, it's this: What's normally done in class, the direct instruction piece, the lecture, is done now at home with videos. And in class, you, the teacher, help students as they do what they would normally do at home.

So it's homework in school and lesson at home? When you are stuck in the old model, kids would go home and do one of three things. If they didn't understand what they were supposed to have learned in school, they gave up, called a friend or cheated. In the flipped classroom, the teacher is there to help with the instruction piece, the learning, while the lecture is done at home.[17]

Al von Halle, an electrical engineer, stands over a waist-high twisted silver metal tube — his unfinished masterpiece — and says, "In the grand scheme of things, $80 million is not that much." That's how much in federal funding his employer, the Princeton Plasma Physics Laboratory, would need to finish the device lying in three big pieces on a concrete floor. The thing has a stirring name: It's a stellerator, or "starmaker," designed to generate and contain a whirling, sputtering bit of the material that makes up the sun — superhot plasma.

Left incomplete in 2008 after running over its $75 million budget, the stellerator was supposed to be the next step in the United States' long-running effort to develop a clean, nearly inexhaustible source of energy: nuclear fusion.

The cousin to nuclear fission — the force behind today's nuclear power plants — fusion produces energy by smashing atoms together instead of splitting them apart. It's the force that drives the sun and the stars, which spit out heat and light when hydrogen atoms collide and fuse. Fusion power — if it can ever be made to work — holds all the cards over fission.

Six decades later, scientists at the lab Spitzer founded are worried that, as China, South Korea, Japan and Europe ramp up their investment in fusion research, the United States is backing away from his dream.[18]

Immigration from Latin America has dropped so precipitously that Asians now outnumber Hispanics among new arrivals in the United States, a new study shows.

The switchover has been in place since at least 2009, according to the Pew Research Center, and is primarily the result of plunging immigration from Mexico, the birthplace of more U.S. immigrants than any other country. This year, Pew said more Mexicans may be leaving the United States than arriving for the first time since the Great Depression, due to weakness in the U.S. job market, a rise in deportation and a decline in Mexico's birthrate.

Currently, the nation's 18 million Asians make up 6 percent of the U.S. population, including multiracial people. More than eight in 10 come from just six countries — China, the Philippines, India, Vietnam, South Korea and Japan. By comparison, the nation's 52 million Hispanics make up almost 17 percent of the population.

Mark Krikorian, executive director of the Center for Immigration Studies, which opposes the Dream Act that would make legal some immigrants who came to the United States as children, said most Americans won't even notice that Asians outnumber Hispanics as new arrivals.[19]

—————————

But it's questionable whether those youths will be able to find work when they get a PhD. Although jobs in some high-tech areas, especially computer and petroleum engineering, seem to be booming, the market is much tighter for lab-bound scientists — those seeking new discoveries in biology, chemistry and medicine.

One big driver of that trend: Traditional academic jobs are scarcer than ever. Once a primary career path, only 14 percent of those with a PhD in biology and the life sciences now land a coveted academic position within five years, according to a 2009 NSF survey. That figure has been steadily declining since the 1970s, said Paula Stephan, an economist at Georgia State University who studies the scientific workforce. *The reason: The supply of scientists has grown far faster than the number of academic positions.*

Since 2004, federal research spending across all agencies has stagnated relative to inflation, according to an analysis by the American Association for the Advancement of Science.

Like many scientists, Amaral grew disillusioned with the system that left her with an expensive degree but few job options. Haas, the former drug company chemist, has even harsher words. She plans to "get out of Jersey and get out of science" when her daughter graduates from high school in two years. "She's very good at everything, very smart," Haas said of her daughter. "She loves chemistry, loves math. I tell her, 'Don't go into science.' I've made that very clear to her."[20]

—————————

A majority of the nation's children will be minorities before the decade is out, crossing a demographic milestone more quickly than previously predicted, according to a new analysis of census statistics by a demographer with the Brookings Institution.

Latinos already are the largest minority among schoolchildren nationwide. One in five students overall is Latino; among kindergarteners, it's one in four. They lag behind other children in achievement, with half never finishing high school.

During Weast's 10 years as superintendant, the district has gone from 50 percent white to 35 percent white, with the largest growth among Latino and African American students. But test scores are higher than ever, he noted. "I see the culture of diversity as an asset," he said. "Don't be afraid of it. Run towards it, embrace it. Not only does it work, it works positively."[21]

———————————

Nationwide, the percentage of Asian American students scoring in the upper echelons on math exams was 17 points higher than the percentage of white students. Notably, that gap has continued to widen in more recent years. In Virginia, for example, Asian American students' advanced-level math performance leapt from 59 percent to 76 percent between 2006 and 2009, compared with an increase from 43 percent to 58 percent for white students.

"The lesson for other groups is that effort counts. Asian American students are working harder, doing better and getting ahead," said Jack Jennings, president of the Center on Education Policy.[22]

———————————

America *is* worse off than it was 30 years ago — in infrastructure, education and research. The country spends much less on infrastructure as a percentage of gross domestic product (GDP). By 2009, federal funding for research and development was half the share of GDP that it was in 1960. Even spending on education and training is lower as a percentage of the federal budget than it was during the 1980s.

The result is that we're falling behind fast. In 2001, the World Economic Forum ranked U.S. infrastructure second in the world. In its latest report we were 24th. The United States spends only 2.4 percent of GDP on infrastructure, the Congressional Budget Office noted in 2010. Europe spends 5 percent; China, 9 percent. In the 1970s, America led the world in the number of college graduates; as of 2009, we were 14th among the countries tracked by the Organization for Economic Cooperation and Development. Annual growth for research and development spending — private and public — was 5.8 percent between 1996 and 2007; in South Korea it was 9.6 percent; in Singapore, 14.5 percent; in China, 21.9 percent.

In other words, the great shift in the U.S. economy over the past 30 years has not been an increase in taxes and regulations but, rather, a decline in investment in human and physical capital.[23]

Today, we are much more rigid about immigrants. We divide newcomers into two categories: legal or illegal, good or bad. We hail them as Americans in the making, or brand them as aliens fit for deportation. That framework has contributed mightily to our broken immigration system and the long political paralysis over how to fix it. We don't need more categories, but we need to change the way we think about categories. We need to look beyond strict definitions of legal and illegal. To start, we can recognize the new birds of passage, those living and thriving in the gray areas. We might then begin to solve our immigration challenges.

Crop pickers, violinists, construction workers, entrepreneurs, engineers, home health-care aides and particle physicists are among today's birds of passage. They are energetic participants in a global economy driven by the flow of work, money and ideas. They prefer to come and go as opportunity calls them. They can manage to have a job in one place and a family in another.

With or without permission, they straddle laws, jurisdictions and identities with ease. We need them to imagine the United States as a place where they can be productive for a while without committing themselves to staying forever. We need them to feel that home can be both here and there and that they can belong to two nations honorably.

If we accept that there are spaces between legal and illegal, then options multiply.

By insisting that immigrants are either Americans or aliens, we make it harder for some good folks to come and we oblige others to stay for the wrong reasons. Worse, we ensure that there will always be people living among us who are outside the law and that it is not good for them or us.[24]

According to the U.S. Bureau of Labor Statistics, in the next five years STEM jobs are expected to grow 21.4 percent, compared with 10.4 percent overall job growth.

The need to further develop STEM education stretches beyond improving math and science scores of American students; it is a matter of national security and a cornerstone for America's economic development.[25]

And then, September 11 happened. The U.S. started to close the doors to educated people. Obtaining the student visa became harder and harder and the cap for an H1B work visa was brought down by Congress. While the U.S. was closing the doors to the scholars and professionals, other countries like Canada and Australia opened their doors. Outsourcing of services to India and manufacturing to China made a bright market for bright graduates.[26]

National standards also appear to be garnering widespread support. Led by the National Governors Association, a "Common Core" of 48 states (Alaska and Texas are the holdouts) is drafting goals that every grade will be expected to meet. Setting a high bar for high school graduation helped raise Massachusetts students from slightly above average to worldbeaters, says Paul Reville, the Massachusetts secretary of education. The Bay State's fourth graders recently scored second in the world on standardized science tests, topping Russia, Taiwan, and other powerhouses.

Research shows that disadvantaged kids typically get the worst teachers-the least trained and the rejects from good schools. The Obama administration wants to change that by encouraging alternative training programs such as Teach for America and improving the caliber of principals, who are responsible for selecting and training teachers. Plans to spend hundreds of millions of dollars to help districts link teacher compensation and .... to student performance.

No Child Left Behind represents a continuation of a 45-year federal commitment to improving the education of poor children. The law's greatest achievement was insisting that data on student achievement be broken down and reported by subgroups, focusing the attention of educators and policymakers right where it belongs: on the troubling and persistent gaps in achievement among poor, minority, English language learning, and special-needs students. For too long, the performance of these groups was masked by overall achievement, but the law pulled the curtain back, demonstrated long suspected gaps, and demanded improvement.

In her quest to revive Washington's public school system, Chancellor Michelle Rhee is pushing innovative but contentious ideas, one of which has garnered her national attention: whether teacher pay can be tied directly to student performance.

The repercussions of Rhee's succeeding, even in incremental fashion, are far-reaching. If she is able to pay District of Columbia teachers based on the academic achievements of their students, she could revolutionize the way public school systems are run across the country.

In New Orleans, home of the most charter schools per child in the country, advertisements for the vast array of available educational options compete for attention with everything from "Lost Pet" fliers to signs for political campaigns. ... In the 2009-2010 school year, these privately run, publically funded hybrids are serving a staggering 61% of all students, up from 57% in 2008-2009. New Orleans is the first major city in the nation with the majority of its students in charters.[27]

––––––––––––––––

This year, $4.3 billion in Race to the Top stimulus funds is available to states that enact reforms tying teacher pay to student achievement and removing caps on the number of charters. This, in turn, has sent state lawmakers scrambling to alter legislation in order to be eligible for funding.

In that context, New Orleans has become the crucible for, the charter movement's ultimate failure or success. So far, the numbers show it has been mostly successful. A recent Stanford University study highlighted Louisiana as one of five states where charter schools outperform traditional public schools. Louisiana Superintendent of Education Paul Pastorek reports that in New Orleans, the combined district test scores have risen 24 percent since 2005, when most students attended traditional schools." However, the study, which uses data from 15 states and the District of Columbia, paints a different picture of the charter movement nationally. According to the study, charters performed slightly worse overall than traditional schools and did worse by black and Hispanic students. Charters did do better by impoverished children.

If the free-market argument for charters is to be borne out--that students benefit when schools compete and that the best schools will rise to the top and the rest will shut down for lack of enrollment--the consumers, or parents, need to understand what exactly they're investing in.

A study in August by Gallup and Phi Delta Kappa International, a public school advocacy group, found that 64 percent of U.S. adults support the charter push, up from 51 percent a year ago. But more than half of the 1,003 surveyed did know that charters are public schools.[28]

––––––––––––––––

Their courses that would intimidate many a college freshman: DNA science, quantum physics, neurobiology. But the students at Thomas Jefferson High School for Science and Technology in Alexandria, Va.-America's top high school for the third consecutive year-take the plunge with enthusiasm.

U.S. News this year examined more than 21,000 public high schools across the country to find out which ones were best preparing their students for success in college. The top performers ranged from high schools such as TJ and New York's Stuyvesant-nationally celebrated high schools that attract recruiters from top colleges-to those with lesser resources like Nashville's Martin Luther King and Hume-Fogg magnet schools. Despite their differences in student bodies, neighborhoods, and histories, each of them has found just the right chemistry to help students grow.[29]

Last fall's release of an annual government report on emigration and immigration set in bold relief the extent of the so-called "brain drain." In 2005, a record 144,815 Germans left the country for lives-and livelihoods-in other nations, a 32.3 percent jump from 2001. And the widespread perception, based on a plethora of anecdotal accounts, is that many of those new expatriates are highly trained professionals. Meanwhile, just 128,100 Germans returned from overseas, 50,000 fewer than the year before.

For industries that rely heavily on engineers (and most do) the brain drain is exacerbating an already acute shortage of talent. There are about 1 million engineers working in Germany yet 20 percent of engineering job openings go unfilled. That currently translates to around 22,000 vacancies. Most large corporations, including DaimlerChrysler, Siemens and Bosch, can still attract most of the engineering talent they need, says Sven Renkel, spokesman for the Association of German Engineers (VDI), because they can offer fatter paychecks and are nationally known.

Schools turned out 37,000 engineering graduates in 2004, 25 percent fewer than in 1996. A brief spike in enrollments should bump up those totals in the short term; but in 2005, enrollments resumed their downward drift.

Ironically, among the millions of unemployed Germans are 65,000 engineers "High unemployment and labor shortages can coincide," observes Heinkaus of the Chambers of Industry and Commerce. "There is no exception concerning engineers". Often, the jobless can't fill vacancies because their talents don't match the company's needs. "You can't change a construction engineer into an aerospace engineer" Renkel wryly notes.[30]

Herein lies a major challenge: How to develop and cultivate great STEM teachers? U.S. schools currently fail to teach STEM effectively. Evidence includes the low standing of US students in international comparisons; for example, in the 2006 Program for International Student Assessment (PISA, conducted by the Organization for Economic Cooperation and Development), American 15- year-olds ranked 24th out of 57 countries in science and 32nd in mathematics.

Many elementary school teachers studied no science or math beyond high school and may remember only that they disliked the subject. Secondary school STEM teachers who were educated decades ago are unlikely to be familiar with modem scientific knowledge. Most troubling, many secondary school classes are taught by teachers with no STEM qualifications at all. The U.S. scientific community has largely ignored the problem of ill- prepared STEM teachers.

Last but not least, STEM professionals must engage actively with precollege-level STEM teachers in a sustained way. In his memoirs, physicist and Nobel Peace Prize recipient Andrei Sakharov describes his father, a high-school physics teacher, as a physicist. STEM teachers must similarly be considered vital members of' the professional scientific community.[31]

It's absurd to argue, as does Texas Gov. Rick Perry (R), that geography should define a child's knowledge. The establishment of clear; tough standards is an important step in better preparing students-and America-for the global economy of the 21st century.[32]

In an interview on NPR (3/29), Michael Martin spoke with Shirley Jackson, president of Rensselaer Polytechnic Institute. They discussed being a woman in a male-dominated field. Jackson is the first African-American woman to run a top research university. Martin questioned why "the presence of women in the sciences seem to lag, especially in the US." Jackson said she thinks there "is something in terms of early exposure to and persistence in math. These are very important things for providing the background for a woman to be in science." She said that working in science requires "working in a lab and some people may find that constraining. But the overall work-life balance is one that any woman who's in a field that is very demanding and high-powered will face." Jackson argued that "those who are in leadership positions for institutions that employ scientists and engineers have to themselves set a tone at the top, as well as having more family-friendly policies".[33]

––––––––––––––

At a time when many "Made in the USA" products struggle in the global marketplace, American diplomas are more coveted than ever. More than 650,000 international students were enrolled in U.S. colleges and universities in 2009, fueling a nearly $18 billion international education industry. Federal government data show that 35,000 foreign students attend primary or secondary schools in the United States, not including one-year cultural exchange programs or short-term language courses.[34]

––––––––––––––

Most of Thursday's changes were less drastic than those made earlier this year. Those included deemphasizing Thomas Jefferson, requiring students to study Jefferson Davis's inaugural address alongside Abraham Lincoln's, and saying that Sen. Joseph McCarthy was justified in his 1950s search for Communist infiltration in American society.

But some of the latest revisions were still hard-fought. Students will now study "efforts by global organizations to undermine U.S. sovereignty, … A standard of studying the solvency of Social Security and Medicare.…"

Paige, who was superintendent of Houston's schools before taking over the Education Department in President George W. Bush's first term, said the school board's decisions were doing damage to the state's education system.[35]

––––––––––––––

The Chronicle of Higher Education (7/6, Blumenstyk) reports, "Three quarters of the patents at top patent-producing American universities had at least one foreign-born inventor."[36]

––––––––––––––

There is a worldwide shortage of people with the qualifications needed by the companies gearing up to meet demand for an estimated 20,000 aircraft in the next 20 years.

Tom Enders, CEO of Airbus parent EADS NV, noted that "the pool of talents in Europe at least has clearly become too small." Airbus says that of 12,000 jobs available in the sector in Europe last year, only 9,000 were filled. At Chicago-based Boeing Co., human resources executive Rick Stephens told AFP that the United States produced 72,000 to 74,000 engineering graduates a year, but "we don't see enough students completing engineering degrees to be able to fill what we believe will be the needs" of the aerospace industry. Thierry Baril, his counterpart at Airbus and EADS, said: "We must fight like hell on the international market to get the best talents." When Boeing closes a factory -- as it did this year in Wichita, Kan. -- putting engineers on the market, "everybody pounds after them, Airbus and Bombardier," Baril said. "It's a little war for talent."[37]

[Remarks by Fareed Zakaria]

So how are we doing? Let's take a rough look. One hundred representative American kids entering high school. What does fate have in store for them? Twenty-five out of that 100 won't graduate from high school. A total of 50 won't go to college. That's half the class that won't go on to higher education. Fifty will attend college, but only 22 will graduate within six years.

On a recent international test, U.S. students ranked only 15th in the world in reading, 23rd in science and 31st in math. Overall, the World Economic Forum ranks the quality of our education at 26th. What's odd is that we've been outspending most developed countries by a long shot. In 2007, we spent over $10,000 per student versus the $7400 average for rich countries. How can we spend so much money and have so little to show for it?

[Referring to Finland, with no standardized testing and a shorter school day], Teaching is a highly respected profession here, on par with doctors and lawyers. That's because they're all required to have master's degrees. The competition for those degrees is fierce. Only one in 10 applicants is accepted to primary schoolteacher training programs. Christy Lanka, Professor of Educational Psychology, University of Helsinki: The elementary teacher program is hardest to get in than the university. It's harder to get in than medical school or law school.[38]

The ranks of America's poor are on track to climb to levels unseen in nearly half a century, erasing gains from the war on poverty in the 1960s amid a weak economy and fraying government safety net.

The analysts' estimates suggest that some 47 million people in the U.S., or 1 in 6, were poor last year. An increase of one-tenth of a percentage point to 15.2 percent would tie the 1983 rate, the highest since 1965. The highest level on record was 22.4 percent in 1959, when the government began calculating poverty figures.[39]

Many prominent studies have sounded the alarm that we are underproducing STEM talent. Those arguing that we have persistent shortages have set the tone of the debate. However, determining whether or not we are producing enough STEM workers to meet demand is fraught with complications. Many students who have adequate math scores to pursue STEM majors are choosing other disciplines.

But it is not only American companies that go abroad—in fact, companies from abroad are also interested in the American workforce and are increasingly "in-sourcing" STEM work. Tata Technologies, an Indian company, announced in late 2010 that they would hire 400 engineers by January to work with their car-manufacturing clients in Detroit, nearly doubling their U.S. employment. In 2011, Tata Consultancy Services announced it is adding 1,200 people between March of 2011 and March of 2012 to its U.S. workforce. Likewise, Infosys Technologies, another Indian firm, plans to hire 1,000 workers over the course of the year.[40]

It turns out, teenagers aren't avoiding careers in engineering because they think it's geeky. They're simply unaware of what engineers do, a [Intel sponsored] survey of 1,000 teenagers showed ... The Intel survey showed 63 percent of the students ages 13 to 18 have never considered the career despite having "generally positive opinions of engineers and engineering."[41]

The workforce pipeline of elementary school teachers fails to ensure that the teachers who inform children's early academic trajectories have the appropriate knowledge of and disposition toward math-intensive subjects and mathematics itself. Prospective teachers can typically obtain a license to teach elementary school without taking a rigorous college-level STEM class such as calculus, statistics, or chemistry, and without demonstrating a solid grasp of mathematics knowledge, scientific knowledge, or the nature of scientific inquiry.[42]

Compared to White students, Black children were less likely to come from a family with both parents in the home, spent more hours watching television, were read to by their parents for fewer hours, and were more likely to be absent from school.[43]

In many cases, Hispanic children were more likely than White children to be raised in circumstances associated with below average academic performance—lack of two parents in the home, for example, or low family income, or access to quality day care.[44]

Most parents think that the science and math classes that their kids take are "just fine," according to a survey of 1,400 Americans, including 646 parents of K-12 students, conducted by Public Agenda and funded by the GE Foundation. Only 42 percent said they felt their kids should take advanced math and science courses, like calculus and physics. And 70 percent said science teaching could be put off until high school. That's a perception problem that needs to be overcome, explains Jean Johnson, Public Agenda's education insights director.[45]

University Leaders on Immigration, a Letter sent to the leaders of the Maryland Senate and the House

[Remarks of Wallace D. Loh of UMCP and Freeman A. Hrabowski III of UMBC among others]

American academic research has benefited from the fact that the US remains a top magnet for the world's best and brightest students and graduates 16 percent of all PhDs worldwide in scientific and technical fields. In 2009, students on temporary visas were 45 percent of all graduate students in engineering, math, computer science and physical sciences-earning 43 percent of all master's degrees and 52 percent of all PhDs. New research shows that in 2011, foreign-born investors were credited contributors on more than 75 percent of patents issued to the top

10 patent-producing universities in the United States-irrefutable proof of the important role immigrants play in American innovation. These inventions lead to new companies and new jobs for American workers, and are an enormous boon to our economy.

But after we have trained and educated these future job creators, our antiquated immigration laws turn them away to work for competitors in other countries. Low limits on visas leave immigrants with no way to stay or facing untenable delays for a permanent visa. Top engineers from India and China face wait times of up to 9 years to get a permanent visa, and new applicants from these countries may face considerably longer waits. And while we turn away these American-educated, trained and funded scientists and engineers, there is a growing skill gap across America's industries. One quarter of US science and engineering firms already report difficulty hiring, and the problem will only worsen: the US is projected to face a shortfall of 230,000 qualified advanced-degree workers in scientific and technical fields by 2018.

The U.S. cannot afford to wait to fix our immigration system. Even as we send away highly skilled workers trained at American universities, competing economies are welcoming these scientists and engineers with streamlined visa applications and creating dedicated visas to ensure that the foreign students who graduate from their own universities can stay and contribute to the local economy. We ask you to work together to develop a bipartisan solution that ensures our top international graduates have a clear path to a green card, so they can stay and create new American jobs. Recent polls show that there is a broad, bipartisan support for this reform, and that the American people want our leaders in Washington to act. Now is the time to do so and ensure that the US remains the world's leading home for innovators.[46]

Brian Caffo teaches a public-health course at Johns Hopkins University that he calls a "mathematical biostatistics boot camp." It typically draws a few dozen graduate students. Never more than 70.

This fall, Caffo was swarmed. He had 15,000 students. They included Patrycja Jablonska in Poland, Ephraim Baron in California, Mohammad Hijazi in Lebanon and many others far from Baltimore who ordinarily would not have a chance to study at the elite Johns Hopkins Bloomberg School of Public Health. They logged on to a Web site called Coursera and signed up. They paid nothing for it.

These students, a sliver of the more than 1.7 million who have registered with Coursera since April, reflect a surge of interest this year in free online learning that could reshape higher education. The phenomenon puts big issues on the table: the growth of tuition, the role of a professor, the definition of a student, the value of a degree and even the mission of universities. "Massive open online courses" or MOOCs, have caught fire in academia.[47]

Reading scores on the SAT for the high school class of 2012 reached a four-decade low, putting a punctuation mark on a gradual decline in the ability of college-bound teens to read passages and answer questions about sentence structure, vocabulary and meaning on the college entrance exam.

Many experts attribute the continued decline to record numbers of students taking the test, including about one-quarter from low-income backgrounds. There are many factors that can affect how well a student scores on the SAT, but few are as strongly correlated as family income.

Scores among every racial group except for those of Asian descent declined from 2006 levels. A majority of test takers -57 percent - did not score high enough to indicate likely success in college, according to the College Board, the organization that administers the test.[48]

[Remarks by Former Florida governor Jeb Bush]
"We say that every child in America has an equal opportunity. Tell that to a kid in whose classroom learning isn't respected. Tell that to a parent stuck in a school where there is no leadership. Tell that to a young, talented teacher who just got laid off because she didn't have tenure. The sad truth is that equality of opportunity doesn't exist in many of our schools. We give some kids a chance, but not all. That failure is the great moral and economic issue of our time. And it's hurting all of America. I believe we can meet this challenge. We need to set high standards for students and teachers and provide students and their parents the choices they deserve. The first step is a simple one. We must stop pre-judging children based on their race, ethnicity or household income. We must stop excusing failure in our schools and start rewarding improvement and success. We must have high academic standards that are benchmarked to the best in the world. All kids can learn."[49]

From planes to PCs to Kevlar, the sun never sets on the products of American ingenuity. But the original engine of U.S. innovation-STEM education-is no longer world class. A half century after the start of the space race, the nation that put a man on the moon faces a gathering storm of faltering schools and squeezed budgets that undermine its competitiveness. Once a world leader in the proportion of its citizenry with college degrees, the United States has fallen to ninth place. Foreign firms now earn a majority of U.S. patents. In 2009, 55 percent of US engineering doctorates went to foreign nationals.

Mention Finland, and most Americans think of Sibelius symphonies or today's popular Angry Birds mobile-phone game. The country enjoys another claim to fame, however: world-class K-12 education. Only a handful of nations come close to matching Finland in math, science and literacy, and non boasts such uniformly high achievement rates across regions and income levels. If American students could match their Finnish peers, McKinsey & Co. estimate, the US economy would be 9 to 16 percent larger and generate as much as $2.3 trillion more annually. How could a nation of 5.5 million people and 2 million saunas produce 15-year-olds on par with Asia's whiz kids?[50]

Published 70 years ago in *Mechanical Engineering* magazine
Past and Future Education of Engineers
By C.E. MacQuigg, Dean, College of Engineering, The Ohio State University, Columbus

By and large, the education of the engineer has been conservative, and the reasons for this are obvious. Quite properly it has been a tradition of engineering education that facts and not fancies must be adhered to. Without a doubt, those men who formed the mold of our engineering philosophy ... held the highest standards of intellectual honesty.

Fortunately, it was unthinkable to them to temporize with untried theories, and naturally the men whom they trained as engineering educators carry this philosophy in turn to their students, thus handing down the tradition of stability…

Another reason for conservatism in engineering education is that technical progress has been dependent not only upon ideas but upon the existence of facts. Since facts are sometimes slow to accumulate, the engineer has been at a disadvantage with respect to the more rapid progress seemingly made in certain nontechnical areas....

Lest engineering educators fall into the danger of smugness, they must recognize a tendency to over-conservatism. Much has been said by competent authorities-not all of it to be accepted as incontrovertible-against the seeming narrowness of technical education today. For example, the exclusion of so-called "cultural" subjects from engineering is decried and the plea that engineering is a culture is not too convincing in this argument. We find two hostile camps today. In one, the engineers who look with disdain on the crowd of armchair philosophers, and in the other, the humanists who in turn scoff at the engineers' stolid mien.[51]

The researchers studied 433 British secondary school children to determine whether mathematics anxiety has an effect on mathematics performance by boys and by girls. The team controlled for test anxiety, a related phenomenon but one that isn't typically controlled for in mathematics anxiety studies, Szucs said.

Children with higher mathematics anxiety have lower mathematics performance, the study found. But girls showed higher levels of mathematics anxiety than boys and anxiety more significantly affected girls' performance than boys' performance, the study noted.

This suggests that girls have the potential to perform better in math if taught to control their anxiety. "Mathematics anxiety warrants attention in the classroom because it could have negative consequences for later mathematics education."

"Mathematics anxiety could account for why only 7 percent of pupils in the United Kingdom study mathematics at A level and why the number of students taking math at university level is in decline," Szucs said. [52]

Both India and China have intense national testing programs to find the brightest students for their elite universities. The competition, the preparation and the national anxiety about the outcomes make the SAT testing programs in the U.S. seem like the minor leagues. The stakes are higher in China and India. The "chosen ones"—those who rank in the top 1%—get their choice of university, putting them on a path to fast-track careers, higher incomes and all the benefits of an upper-middle-class life.

The system doesn't work so well for the other 99%. There are nearly 40 million university students in China and India. Most attend institutions that churn out students at low cost. Students complain that their education is "factory style" and "uninspired." Employers complain that many graduates need remedial training before they are fully employable.

For now, the U.S. university system is still far ahead. But over the next decade, there will be a global competition to educate the next generation, and China and India have the potential to change the balance of power. With large pools of qualified students coming of age, the two countries have made reforming their universities a top priority.[53]

The day after 33 Chilean miners were brought safely to the surface after being trapped underground for 70 days, a newspaper story carried the headline: "Chile's Rescue Formula: 75% Science, 25% Miracle". But the headline misquoted the topographer who had directed the drilling that located the miners. What she actually had said was even quoted in the body of the article: "It was 75 percent engineering and 25 percent miracle. Did the headline writer see science where engineering was clearly said and meant? Did the headline writer really believe that science and engineering are equivalent?"

Engineering is not a synonym for science; it is more than science. Had science alone been relied upon to rescue the miners, they might still be there. Science is about studying what is; engineering is about doing something about things as we find them. Engineering may exploit scientific knowledge in seeking solutions to problems, but engineering is about going beyond science into the realm of design.[54]

"If math and science seem boring and of no use on a primary education level, who would want to pursue it while in college?" he [Allen Gordon] says. "Especially when you don't see many, if any, black men or women teaching. Math and science are not something that black men and women sit around and pontificate about at home, dinner parties, the sports bar, hair salon, et cetera," he says. "It doesn't fit into their social idea of status. Let's face it, there is no glory in saying, 'I teach math or science.' Career school teachers still seem to be very proletarian."

Money is another factor in the STEM disparity. It takes many years after college to get the advanced degrees needed to become leaders in math and science fields – university professors, directors of research labs, heads of engineering departments – and some black students can't afford to wait that long. Before one recent New Year's Eve, Smith, the Johns Hopkins student, was debating whether to purchase a bus ticket from Baltimore to New York City to hang out with friends. It was a tough decision – the ticket cost $37. Smith, 27, received a fellowship for black scientists this year from Merck and the United Negro College Fund. As he works toward his PhD, Smith lives on a salary and stipend of about $25,000 per year. But he's still several years away from completing his PhD, and he's tired of agonizing over a $37 bus ticket. Even after he gets that degree, he'll need to do a year of post-doctoral study. "If I stay here at Hopkins" for post-doc work, he says, "I'll make the same or less than a city sanitation worker." At each stage of science education, many black students feel pressure to stop studying and start earning real money. Smith, who has an undergraduate degree from MIT, says he could be making as much as $115,000 per year in a corporate job.

Mae Jemison [the first black female astronaut] identifies another incentive. Even though scientists may use the same methodology, "what topics they choose to research, even the interpretation of facts or what they choose to look at is influenced by experience. So many times it's the diversity of thought and perception and experience base that starts to make the difference in the problems you research and the solutions you consider," she says. "It's a much more robust reason for diversity that just the head count."[55]

References

1. Wai, J. (25 March 2012). Finding the Next Einstein. *Psychology Today*. Retrieved from <http://www.psychologytoday.com/blog/finding-the-next-einstein/201203/why-is-it-socially-acceptable-be-bad-math>
2. Remarks by the President at the 2010 National Medal of Science and National Medal of Technology and Innovation Ceremony. (November 17).
3. National Academies Press (2012). *Lifelong Learning Imperative in Engineering: Sustaining American Competitiveness in the 21st Century.*
4. Committee on the Evaluation Framework for Successful K-12 STEM Education Board on Science Education and Board on Testing and Assessment Division of Behavioral and Social Sciences and Education. (November 2012). *Monitoring Progress Toward Successful K-12 STEM Education: A Nation Advancing?.*
5. Gewertz, C. (7 November 2012). Final College-Readiness Definition Guides Test Consortium. *Education Week*. Retrieved from <http://blogs.edweek.org/edweek/curriculum/2012/11/final_college_readiness_defini.html>
6. Remarks of Richard D. Stephens, Senior Vice President for Human Resources and Administration, The Boeing Company. Retrieved from <http://www.fednet.net/nae100112/>

7. Remarks of Dr. Linda P. Katehi, Chancellor of University of California, Davis. Retrieved from <http://www.fednet.net/nae 100112/>

8. Ibid.

9. Zakaria, F. (2012). How government funding of science rewards U.S. taxpayers. *The Washington Post*, 20 June 2012.

10. Michelle Obama, remarks at NSF. Retrieved from <http://blogs.suntimes.com/sweet/2011/09/michelle_obama_pushing _stem_ed.html>

11. White House Forum Features ASME President (2012). *Mechanical Engineering*, June 2012.

12. Pearlstein, S. (2011). Mark Them Tardy to the Revolution. *The Washington Post*, May 29, 2011, p. G5.

13. Dr. Anant Argwal, President, edX and Professor, MIT, NAE 2012 Annual Meeting, Educating Engineers: Preparing 21st century leaders in the context of new modes of learning, September 30, 2012

14. A Case for More Science Time in Grade Schools. *Mechanical Engineering*, January 2012, p. 13.

15. Natarajan, P. (2012). Want More Scientists? Turn Grade Schools into Laboratories. *The Washington Post*, 5 February 2012, p. B2.

16. Knapp, B. (2012). A Case for Optimism. *The Washington Post*, January 16, 2012, p. A15.

17. Strauss, V. (2012). Classwork at Home, Homework in Class. *The Washington Post*, 16 April 2012, p. B2.

18. Vastag, B. (2012). Seeking Star Power. *The Washington Post*, 26 June 2012, p. E1.

19. Morello, C. (2012). Asians Outnumber Hispanics Among New Arrivals to the U.S., Analysis Shows. *The Washington Post*, 19 June 2012, p. A3.

20. Vastag, B. (2012). Scientists Heeded Call but Few Can Find Jobs. *The Washington Post*, 8 July 2012, p. A14.

21. Morello, C. (2011). Demographics Among Children Shifting Quickly. *The Washington Post*, 6 April 2011, p. A18.

22. Sieff, K. (2012). Asian Americans Outpacing Peers. *The Washington Post*, 6 April 2011, p. B5.

23. Zakaria, F. (2012). What Voters Are Really Choosing in November. *The Washington Post*, 19 July 2012.

24. Suro, R. (2012). We See All Immigrants as Legal or Illegal. Big Mistake". *The Washington Post*, 13 July 2012.

25. STEM Education: Pathways to opportunity. *The Washington Post*, 27 June 2012.

26. Faridani, S. (2007). Job Drain: Letters to the Editor. *Mechanical Engineering*, 8 September 2007.